# Agricultural Land Redistribution and Land Administration in Sub-Saharan Africa

DIRECTIONS IN DEVELOPMENT
Agriculture and Rural Development

# Agricultural Land Redistribution and Land Administration in Sub-Saharan Africa

*Case Studies of Recent Reforms*

Frank F. K. Byamugisha, Editor

**THE WORLD BANK**
**Washington, D.C.**

**Library of Congress Cataloging-in-Publication Data**

Agricultural land redistribution and land administration in Sub-Saharan Africa : case studies of recent reforms / edited by Frank F. K. Byamugisha.
     pages cm. — (Directions in development)
     Includes bibliographical references.
ISBN 978-1-4648-0188-4 (alk. paper) — ISBN 978-1-4648-0189-1
     1. Land reform—Africa, Sub-Saharan—Case studies. 2. Land tenure—Africa, Sub-Saharan—Case studies.  I. Byamugisha, Frank. II. World Bank. III. Series: Directions in development (Washington, D.C.)
     HD1333.A357A37 2014
     333.3'167—dc23
                                                                                                    2014008443

# Contents

# Acknowledgments

The bulk of the materials in this book were prepared as a background to a recently published book on land governance in Africa, *Securing Africa's Land for Shared Prosperity* (Byamugisha 2013). Funding was provided by the Africa Regional Studies Program managed by the Office of the Chief Economist of the World Bank's Africa Region and was supplemented by the FAO-World Bank Co-operative Program.

# Contributors

## About the Editor

**Frank F. K. Byamugisha** is a consultant in land, agriculture, and natural resource management after retiring in December 2013 from the World Bank, where he was an operations adviser and lead land specialist in East Asia and Africa, and where he worked for more than 20 years on land tenure and administration reforms, especially in Asia and Africa. Before joining the Bank, he was an assistant secretary at the Ministry of Finance in Papua New Guinea. He holds a PhD in economics and a master of science degree in land surveying from the University of East London; a master's degree in agricultural development economics from the Australian National University; and a bachelor of science degree in agriculture from Makerere University, Uganda.

## About the Contributors

**Rexford A. Ahene** is professor of economics and chair of Africana Studies at Lafayette College, Easton, Pennsylvania, USA.

**John Bruce** is the director of Land and Development Solutions International, a consulting firm based in Alexandria, Virginia, USA. He retired in 2006 from the World Bank where he worked as a senior counsel (Land Law) and land tenure specialist.

**Mykhailo Cheremshynskyi** is an international consultant in Land Administration and Land Information Systems, Kiev, Ukraine.

**Edward Lahiff** is a lecturer at University College, Cork, Ireland.

**Guo Li** is a senior agriculture economist in the Africa Region of the World Bank, Washington, DC, USA.

**Hardwick Tchale** is a senior agriculture economist in the Africa Region of the World Bank, Washington, DC, USA.

# Abbreviations

| | |
|---|---|
| ANC | African National Congress |
| BEE | black economic empowerment (South Africa) |
| CBRLDP | Community-Based Rural Land Development Project (Malawi) |
| CCRO | Certificate of Customary Rights of Occupancy (Tanzania) |
| CLaRA | Communal Land Rights Act (South Africa) |
| CLS | customary land secretariat (Ghana) |
| CNDRA | Center for National Documentation, Records and Archives (Liberia) |
| COC | Community Oversight Committee (Malawi) |
| COWI | COWI Consulting Engineers and Planners AS (of Denmark) |
| CRDP | Comprehensive Rural Development Program (South Africa) |
| CVL | Certificate of Village Land (Tanzania) |
| DFID | Department for International Development (United Kingdom) |
| DLA | Department of Land Affairs (South Africa) |
| DLB | District Land Board (Uganda) |
| DLSC | Department of Lands, Surveys and Cartography (Liberia) |
| DMS | document management system |
| DRDLR | Department of Rural Development and Land Reform (South Africa) |
| DSA | daily subsistence allowance |
| ELAP | Ethiopia Land Administration Project |
| ELTAP | Ethiopian Land Tenure and Administration Project |
| ESTA | Extension of Security of Tenure Act of 1997 (South Africa) |
| FAO | Food and Agricultural Organization (of the United Nations) |
| FLOSS | free/libre open-source software |
| GDP | gross domestic product |
| GIS | geographic information system |
| GPS | Global Positioning System |
| ICT | information and communication technologies |
| LAP | Land Administration Project (Ghana) |

| | |
|---|---|
| LC | Land Commission (Ghana) |
| LIS | Land Information System |
| LRAD | Land Redistribution for Agricultural Development (South Africa) |
| LRMB | Land Rights Management Board (South Africa) |
| LRMC | Land Rights Management Committee (South Africa) |
| LSSP | Land Sector Strategic Plan (Uganda) |
| LUPMIS | Land Use Planning and Management Information System (Ghana) |
| MCC | Millennium Challenge Corporation |
| M&E | monitoring and evaluation |
| MINAGRI | Ministry of Agriculture and Animal Resources (Rwanda) |
| MINIRENA | Ministry of Natural Resources (Rwanda) |
| MLHUD | Ministry of Lands, Housing and Urban Development (Uganda) |
| MLME | Ministry of Land, Mines and Energy (Liberia) |
| NGO | nongovernmental organization |
| OECD | Organisation for Economic Co-operation and Development |
| OSCAR | Open Source Cadastral and Registry (Ghana) |
| PLAS | Proactive Land Acquisition Strategy (South Africa) |
| PPP | public-private partnership |
| PSCP | Private Sector Competitiveness Project |
| RLC | Regional Land Commission (Ghana) |
| SIDA | Swedish International Development Cooperation Agency |
| SLAG | Settlement/Land Acquisition Grant (South Africa) |
| SNNP | Southern Nations, Nationalities, and People's Region (Ethiopia) |
| SPILL | Strategic Plan in Implementation of Land Law (Tanzania) |
| SPLAG | Settlement/Production Land Acquisition Grant (South Africa) |
| SSA | Sub-Saharan Africa |
| ULC | Uganda Land Commission |
| UMLIS | Urban Management Land Information System (Ghana) |
| UNDP | United Nations Development Programme |
| UNHCR | United Nations High Commissioner for Refugees |
| UNLP | Uganda National Land Policy |
| USAID | United States Agency for International Development |
| WMS | workflow management system |
| WSWB | willing seller–willing buyer |
| | |
| R | rand (South Africa) |
| T Sh | Tanzania shillings |
| US$ | U. S. dollar |
| U Sh | Uganda shillings |

# Introduction and Overview of Agricultural Land Redistribution and Land Administration Case Studies

Frank F. K. Byamugisha

The six case studies in this book were prepared as background studies for a synthesis report on land administration and reform in Sub-Saharan Africa (SSA) recently published by the World Bank (Byamugisha 2013). Collectively they cover two main areas of land governance: reforms in redistributing agricultural land and reforms in land administration. The first two case studies discuss reforms in redistributing agricultural land in Malawi and South Africa. Reforms in four thematic areas of land administration are addressed in the remaining case studies, encompassing experience from various countries as follows:

- Decentralizing land administration (Ethiopia, Ghana, Tanzania, and Uganda)
- Developing postconflict land administration systems (Liberia and Rwanda)
- Reengineering and computerizing Land Information Systems (LISs) (Ghana and Uganda) and
- Improving management of government land through land inventories (Ghana and Uganda).

The common elements between sometimes quite disparate experiences provide lessons of relevance to other SSA countries contemplating similar reforms.

This chapter is divided into three sections. The first section defines the problem in land ownership inequality and poor land administration, and the second section addresses the question of why reforms are necessary. The third section provides a brief overview of the six case studies, highlighting their lessons and applicability to other SSA countries.

## The Problems of Land Ownership Inequality and Poor Land Administration

### Land Ownership Inequality

The colonization of Africa included the appropriation of land for white settlers and colonial corporations predominantly in Southern Africa (Angola, Botswana, Malawi, Mozambique, Namibia, South Africa, Swaziland, Zambia, and Zimbabwe), Kenya, and Côte d'Ivoire. Just before and immediately after independence from the late 1950s through the 1970s, several of these countries undertook land reforms to redress colonial and postindependence land ownership inequalities and regressive land use policies. The reforms undertaken included nationalization of the settler and corporate lands (as in Angola, Mozambique, and Zambia) and use of market-based mechanisms for land acquisition and compensation using funds provided by the former colonial masters as agreed to in independence packages (as in Botswana, Kenya, Malawi, Swaziland, and Zimbabwe).

Despite these reforms, inequality in land ownership and landlessness are still at unacceptable levels in many countries. The most extreme example of land ownership inequality is in South Africa. At the end of apartheid in 1994, approximately 82 million hectares of commercial farmland (86 percent of all farmland) were held by the white minority (10.9 percent of the population), concentrated in the hands of approximately 60,000 owners. Notwithstanding a land reform program launched in 1994 to reduce land ownership inequality by transferring land from white South Africans to the majority and poor black population, as of March 2013, nearly 80 percent of the land was overwhelmingly owned by white minorities.[1] In Kenya, three powerful political families are estimated to own more than 1 million acres of rural land, while at least 4 million rural Kenyan citizens are landless and at least 11 million own less than 1 hectare. High levels of land ownership inequality and landlessness are still a major source of conflict in terms of race relations and economic injustices in countries such as South Africa and Zimbabwe, while in others (notably Côte d'Ivoire, Kenya, and Liberia), they represent gross economic and social injustices that threaten the political and economic stability of these countries.

### Poor Land Governance

Postindependence African governments have not invested enough in land administration systems, resulting in decaying surveying infrastructure such as national geodetic networks, reliance on outdated large-scale base maps, and provision of inefficient land administration services in many SSA countries. Observers have noted various symptoms of poor land administration (Byamugisha 2013). First, even half a century after independence, only 10 percent of rural land in SSA is registered; the rest is undocumented and thus vulnerable to land grabbing and expropriation without compensation. Second, increased investor interest in large-scale agriculture in SSA has led to "land grabs," to the extent that millions of hectares of land have been claimed by investors, with poor land governance leading to violations of principles of responsible agro-investment and dispossession of local communities (Cotula et al. 2009; Deininger et al. 2011). Third, land administration is so inefficient that it takes twice as long (65 days) and costs twice as much (9.4 percent of property value) to transfer land in SSA than in Organisation for Economic Co-operation and Development (OECD) countries (31 days; 4.4 percent) (World Bank 2012). Fourth, there is considerable corruption in land administration, as indicated by the Food and Agricultural Organization (FAO) and Transparency International in their study of 61 countries, which found that weak governance had increased the likelihood of corruption in land administration (Arial, Fagan, and Zimmermann 2011). Fifth, capacity and demand in land administration are low relative to the requirements and to countries in other regions. For example, Ghana, Kenya, and Uganda each have fewer than 10 professional land surveyors per 1 million population compared to Malaysia (197) and Sri Lanka (150) (Byamugisha 2013).

## The Need for Agricultural Land Distribution and Land Administration Reforms

### Reforms in Agricultural Land Distribution

Time after time, the world has witnessed peasants dispossessed of their lands through coercion in the Americas, Europe, Asia, and Africa, resulting in highly unequal land distribution often followed by peasant uprisings. In Africa, colonial settlements left such a legacy of unequal land distribution that even independence struggles and negotiations were unable to correct the situation. The operation of land markets amid imperfections in other markets has also left its mark on the formation of highly unequal land distribution. Although the rise of social movements and more progressive governments has led to serious attempts to correct the highly unequal distribution of land, this has been done primarily through government-led compulsory land acquisition (expropriation) and distribution programs, many of which have been slow, administratively costly, and often unaccompanied by measures to develop redistributed land. As a result, the amount of land redistributed has been limited and has led neither to sustainable increases in productivity of the redistributed land nor to reduced poverty of the beneficiaries.[2] In a bid to improve the performance and impacts of land reforms, alternatives to government-led compulsory land reforms were initiated especially during the 1990s. These alternatives have been labeled as market-assisted land reforms, often community based. Both the old-style land acquisition and distribution approach and the alternative mechanisms of land reform were reviewed and reported on in a recent publication (Binswanger-Mkhize, Bourguignon, and van den Brink 2009). The review found encouraging results from the alternative new mechanisms of market-assisted and community-based approaches, especially in Brazil and Malawi, although a more comprehensive review of impacts was recommended to identify successful elements for scaling up.

Given the long history of redistributive land reform and its mixed record of success, it is worthwhile to ask if there is justification for continuing to undertake these reforms. At least three theoretical reasons support the contention that redistributive land reform may lead to greater efficiency and equity: (1) the negative relationship between farm size and productivity can be exploited by land reform, (2) ownership of land that can enable credit access acts as a substitute for insurance to smooth consumption seasonally and over longer cycles for poor people, and (3) the same credit-accessing landownership enables financing of lumpy, indivisible, or long gestation investments for poor people. Indeed, cross- and intracountry studies have empirically confirmed the potential of a better distribution of real property (land) to enhance growth and reduce poverty.

### Negative Relationship between Farm Size and Productivity

Because of large farms' reliance on hired labor (as opposed to small farms which use family labor), they are faced with costs of supervising hired workers and are therefore less productive and often have lower levels of land utilization than small farms. A large body of empirical research backs up this contention (Barraclough 1970; Berry and Cline 1979; Kutcher and Scandizzo 1981; Barrett 1996; Benjamin and Brandt 2002). Thus a redistribution of land from wage-operated large farms to family-run small farms would lead to increases in productivity (Binswanger, Deininger, and Feder 1995). However, a smaller body of empirical research does not find evidence of this inverse relationship (Hill 1972; Kevane 1996; Zaibet and Dunn 1998). More recently, this minority view has received support from Collier and Dercon (2009) who, in the context of African agriculture, argue that this inverse relationship has been supported by only a few studies, with a few others finding a reverse (i.e., positive) farm-size/productivity relationship. It should be noted that most of the earlier research was done to test the main explanation of the inverse relationship, mainly imperfect factor markets—labor, land, and insurance markets (Barrett, Bellemare, and Hou 2010). More recent research that has been done testing other explanatory factors, especially omitted variables (mainly quality of land) and statistical issues, has confirmed the existence of the inverse relationship (Larson et al. 2012; Carletto, Savastano, and Zezza 2013). These research findings are relevant not only for indicating the relevant scale for the desired level of productivity; they are perhaps even more relevant to indicating the relevant scale to optimize achievement of food security and poverty reduction because productivity and incomes from family-operated small farms have a greater impact on the latter when compared with wage-operated large farms.

### Credit-Accessing Landownership, Smoothing of Intertemporal Consumption, and Financing Lumpy Investments

With availability of credit facilities, landownership can enable poor people's access to collateral-based credit, which they can use as a substitute for insurance to sustain consumption across seasons and longer business cycles; the credit enabled by landownership can also be used by the poor to finance indivisible, lumpy, and longer gestation investments such as schooling, farm equipment (such as ox-drawn ploughs and irrigation pumps), and planting of perennial crops (Galor and Zeira 1993; Bardhan, Bowles, and Gintis 2000). Empirical evidence to support these contentions can be found in Jalan and Ravallion (1999) and

Fafchamps and Pender (1997). As such, a redistribution of land from wealthy owners of large farms to land-poor farmers, renters, or farm workers would result in enhanced productivity, economic growth, and poverty reduction and would constitute a more efficient and effective policy instrument for achieving equity than a mere distribution of income (Mookhrjee 1997). But landownership can enhance access to credit only if it is documented and easily verifiable through a public land registry underpinned by a robust LIS as described in the case study in chapter 6 (Deininger and Feder 2009).

### Empirical Evidence Confirming Impact of Better Land Distribution on Growth and Poverty Reduction

Cross-country regressions by Birdsall and Londono (1997) found a significant negative impact of the initial unequal asset distribution on subsequent economic growth, while research by Deininger and Squire (1998) found such an impact to be particularly severe for the poor. It should be noted that these measurements of relationships between land distribution and growth were largely based on correlations, and not causation.

### Reforms in Land Administration

Sound land policies and efficient land administration are critical to economic growth, food security, and poverty alleviation, especially in Africa, where about 80 percent of the population still rely on agriculture for their livelihoods (African Development Bank Group 2010). In fully settled areas where agricultural production increases are no longer feasible through area expansion, enhancing agricultural productivity on existing farms is the only path to agricultural growth. Sound land policies can facilitate growth in agricultural productivity via secure land tenure, which enhances opportunities for investment. For example, land reforms in China in 1978 dismantled collective farming and conferred land rights to households, unleashing a period of prolonged growth in agricultural productivity that transformed rural China. In Africa, impact studies have confirmed that a recent massive land certification program in Ethiopia and an ongoing countrywide registration program in Rwanda have been associated with significant increases in investment (Deininger et al. 2007; Ali, Deininger, and Goldstein 2011).

Sound land policies are also essential for facilitating flows of private investment into agriculture and other land-based industries, including light manufacturing. Although it has long been known that land tenure security is associated with private investment (Place 2009), the recent surges in investor interest in Africa in agriculture (following the 2008 food and commodity price boom) and in oil, mineral resources, and tourism have put a special premium on land tenure security: without it, investors cannot be sure of reaping the full benefits of land deals and investments, nor can local communities receive protection and full compensation for their land rights or a fair share of returns from investments on their land (Deininger et al. 2011).

Outside of the agriculture sector, land is a constraint for most manufacturing firms in SSA (Dinh et al. 2012). Small and large firms setting up or expanding face a lack of access to industrial land equipped with utilities and transport linkages to markets; they also lack land to use as collateral to secure loans. To facilitate growth in manufacturing in SSA, the issue of secure access to land must be tackled head-on.

The role placed on land policies in ensuring social stability in SSA cannot be overemphasized in light of conflicts over land arising from global commercial interests in natural resources (e.g., in the Democratic Republic of Congo, Liberia, and Sierra Leone); and pervasive land disputes associated with access to land by returning refugees and internally displaced people in conflict-afflicted countries, including Burundi, Côte d'Ivoire, Rwanda, Somalia, Republic of South Sudan, and Uganda. Last but not least, sound land policies are required to protect natural resources and the environment against irrational use and pollution. The recent challenges of climate change and the upsurge in investor interest in African agriculture and natural resources make this even more urgent. Growing investments in the extraction of oil and mineral resources and the exploitation of forestry and water resources also call for better land use planning and land tenure policies to ensure sustainable resource use and to avoid pollution. Countermeasures to global warming, such as carbon offset programs of reforestation, require documentation of land rights to identify and secure the rights of tree plantation owners involved in these programs.

## Case Studies in Redistributive Land Reform in Malawi and South Africa

### Redistributive Land Reform in Malawi

To address the highly unequal distribution of its overcrowded arable land, which coexists with underutilized large-scale farms, Malawi piloted a land reform program in 2004 with funding from the World Bank (2004). The pilot project aimed to increase the income of about 15,000 rural poor families through a decentralized, community-based, and voluntary approach in four districts, modeled on Brazil's market-based approach to land reform (under implementation since the mid-1990s). The pilot had three key elements: (1) voluntary acquisition by communities of land sold by willing estate owners; (2) resettlement and on-farm development, including transportation of settlers, establishment of shelter, and purchase of basic inputs and necessary advisory services; and (3) survey and registration of redistributed land. Land reform beneficiaries, organized in voluntary groups, were self-selected on the basis of predefined eligibility criteria. Each family received a grant of US$1,050, managed directly by beneficiaries, of which up to 30 percent was for land acquisition, and the rest for transportation, water, shelter, and farm development. Implementation was decentralized through District Assembly institutions and required capacity enhancement, especially for surveying and registration.

According to impact evaluation studies, the project achieved impressive results, including an increase of 40 percent in agricultural incomes for beneficiaries (compared to nonbeneficiaries) between 2005/06 and 2008/09, an economic rate of return of 20 percent, and positive impacts on the livelihoods of beneficiaries and surrounding communities, with improvements in land holdings, land tenure security, crop production, and productivity, and consequently on income and food security (Simtowe, Mangisoni, and Mendola 2011). These results leave no doubt that Malawi's redistributive land reform model is one upon which SSA countries can build to address land ownership inequality and landlessness. Key lessons learned are the following:

- Community-driven land redistribution programs are possible and can be economically viable in SSA.
- Capping the maximum amount of the beneficiary grant that can be spent on land acquisition, but allowing flexibility to spend grant money on resettlement and land/farm development, is an effective mechanism to encourage beneficiaries to seek and negotiate for lower priced land.
- The market-assisted willing seller–willing buyer (WSWB) approach is generally effective, but may not work if there are no taxes (ground rent) on land, if taxes are very low and/or poorly enforced, or if large-scale agriculture is subsidized through freehold land (as in Malawi).
- Land reform programs should be embedded within broader programs of rural development to ensure that beneficiaries are able to optimize the benefits of such programs.

### Redistributive Land Reform in South Africa

South Africa has had perhaps the greatest urgency for land reform. Unlike in Malawi, land reform in South Africa has made slow progress in reducing ownership inequality and has had minimal impact on productivity and incomes, as discussed in the first section of this chapter. The case study on South Africa concludes that its land reform program is missing two important aspects that would enable it to make a significant impact on the livelihoods of beneficiaries. First, there is no viable small-farmer path to development, which could enable the millions of households residing in communal areas and on commercial farms to expand their own production and accumulate wealth and resources in an incremental manner. This requires radical restructuring of existing farm units to create family-size farms, more realistic farm planning, appropriate support from a much-reformed state agricultural service, and a much greater role for beneficiaries in the design and implementation of their own projects. Second, there is an absence of a sustained focus on implementation, resource mobilization, and timely policy adjustment. Nonetheless, the lessons learned for program design and implementation from South Africa's program are the following:

- Market-based land reforms alone do not work. The WSWB approach applied in South Africa since 1994 has not worked partly because owners of large holdings are unwilling to sell because they have high incentives to hold on to the land. Market purchases from "willing sellers" must be supported by genuinely proactive interventions by the state to remove incentives for large holdings and to tax unused land above a certain threshold to enable beneficiaries to purchase land at normal market prices.

Agricultural Land Redistribution and Land Administration in Sub-Saharan Africa
http://dx.doi.org/10.1596/978-1-4648-0188-4

- There is a need for appropriate legislation and its rigorous application to enable land reform to work. For example, legislative action is required to remove legal restrictions against land subdivision, which prevents large-scale farmland from being divided to better suit the farming needs of land reform beneficiaries.
- There is need for stronger involvement of civil society in sensitizing and improving the bargaining capacity of beneficiaries.
- Postsettlement support is critical to ensure the long-term success of land redistribution programs. If the poor are not targeted with grants, as was done in Malawi, a land reform program driven by markets alone is unlikely to reach or benefit the poor.

It should be noted that the Malawi redistributive land reform is the only one in Africa that has been subjected to a systematic impact assessment. To ensure lessons are learned to improve design of future land reforms, more systematic efforts are direly needed to analyze the impacts of land-related interventions at a microlevel and to plan for these assessments at the initial stages of project conceptualization. In the case of Africa, advantage should be taken of more waves of household panel survey data becoming available under the Living Standards Measurement Study–Integrated Surveys on Agriculture initiative.[3] These data sets could be explored to support an increased emphasis on documenting the dynamic effects of land reforms at a microlevel.

## Case Studies in Reforms in Land Administration

### Decentralization of Land Administration

Local institutions often have a better understanding of local needs and are more inclined to respond to them, because they have better access to information and are more easily held accountable to local populations (Ribot 2001; Sikor and Muller 2009). Given that land is ineffably local, the justification for decentralizing land administration is potentially strong; indeed, in much of Africa, land administration is already effectively decentralized to traditional authorities who administer land under custom, with or without a legal foundation in national law. In light of the growing international demand for land, and the associated urgency to provide written records of land rights to rural people, efforts to decentralize are timely.

The extent to which the benefits of land administration decentralization are realized depends on how the process is structured and implemented; local governments are not necessarily more democratic, more efficient, or less corrupt than central governments, and not all land administration functions are best carried out at the local level. Centralized management may be needed to deliver technology, maintain uniform national standards, or ensure quality of services. Local capacity may be difficult to create, or the technology needed may be too complex or expensive to maintain locally. Decentralization requires strategies appropriate to the tasks, objectives, and budget. Recent experience suggests that the cost of creating new local administration capacities is high; some reliance on traditional authorities may be less costly (Bruce and Knox 2009). But the legitimacy of traditional authorities is also eroding rapidly because of pressure from a recent surge in foreign direct investment, significant demand for land for large-scale agriculture, and associated opportunities for corruption (Nolte 2012). There is no one model or process that can ensure success, but a review of what has and has not worked can guide the design of future decentralization.

Ethiopia, Ghana, Tanzania, and Uganda have taken different approaches to decentralization. The case study focuses on the effectiveness of each approach, examining (1) the land administration roles decentralized, and by whom they are performed, (2) the interactions of decentralized land administration institutions and those at higher levels, (3) the interactions of decentralized land administration institutions and other local institutions, particularly those with land management roles, (4) the extent to which the decentralization is a deconcentration or a devolution of authority, and (5) the sustainability of each system in management and financial terms. A number of observations and recommendations regarding decentralization of land administration in SSA emerge, such as the following:

- Land administration decentralization happens within the more general decentralization of government and public services.
- Decentralization can be greatly facilitated if capable community institutions are already in place.
- Decentralization of land administration tasks tends to be deconcentrations of central government authority, partly reflecting the desire to facilitate the functioning of national land markets.
- Initial decentralization of any sophisticated land administration machinery requires a strong central government lead and assistance to communities, although a regional or district lead may suffice for very simple systems.
- Community institutions have an important role in the maintenance and operation of the decentralized system, even when the central government takes a strong lead, especially in the initial identification of holdings and rights holders. Given that local institutional capacity (at local government and community levels) is critical to successful decentralization of local administration, deliberate efforts need to be made to create and strengthen such capacity and to provide resources for ongoing maintenance (Mansuri and Rao 2012). This is necessary to avoid ending up with a very weak decentralized system that cannot withstand stress, such as the continuous creation of new districts as in Uganda where the number of districts doubled from 56 to 112 between 2002 and 2013 (see chapter 3).
- The institutional framework for decentralized land administration should be planned conservatively, with a clear sense of the long-term system maintenance costs and the source of their funding.

### Developing Land Administration in Postconflict Countries

Postconflict countries often experience continuing tensions over land that are grounded in issues that predate the original conflict and may have even contributed to it. Actions taken during the period of conflict can also exacerbate land problems. Dealing decisively with land issues at the cessation of conflict is therefore critical not only to break the vicious cycle of conflict but also to contribute to postconflict economic recovery. Some countries have done this successfully. For example, Cambodia avoided a recurrence of conflict by basing land rights on occupancy, resettling displaced people, and permitting the military to use lands occupied in the war zone until they were demobilized and reintegrated; this contributed to postwar reconstruction as well as to peace (Zimmermann 2002; Torhonen and Palmer 2004). Similarly, Mozambique resettled 5 million people after its peace agreement, using local institutions to mediate and resolve conflicts that emerged, while also working on a new land law that provided a right of occupancy to rural families; these efforts contributed to the country's social and economic stability (Tanner 2002).

One case study herein reviews Rwanda and Liberia's experiences with reestablishing systems of land administration and embarking on needed reforms. In both countries, land issues quickly came to the forefront of postconflict national concerns, and both governments appreciated their seriousness. In addition, development partners made funding available to address them, if somewhat belatedly. At the same time, the ability to cope with policy and management issues was badly degraded by the conflict in both countries, and many years passed before either government could seriously engage in these issues.

In Rwanda, extremely high population pressure on land contributed to the initial conflict and complicates current attempts to appropriate the land of those who fled and to make readjustments for land sharing and resettlement of returned refugees. In Liberia, prewar tensions created by Americo-Liberians' land appropriations persist and are exacerbated by the major population displacement that occurred during the conflict. The two countries took different tracks to develop and implement land reform strategies: Rwanda moved more quickly on systematic registration of land rights, whereas Liberia, arguably taking a more considered approach, focused on policy, law reform, and rebuilding government capacity. At least four lessons emerge from the case study:

- At the end of conflicts, postconflict governments and donors need to focus early not only on conflict management but also on developing basic land policies to address underlying tensions over land.
- Moving more rapidly into policy work after cessation of conflict requires earlier deployment of development partners' expertise on land tenure to assist governments struggling with land policy issues.
- Rebuilding the capacity of governments in land administration and land dispute resolution requires reestablishing technical capacity and retraining staff in the basics of management.
- Where land governance institutions are very weak or simply not present, governments will initially need to resort to institutional approaches such as task forces and special commissions that can bring together limited existing expertise to focus on land matters.

### *Rationalizing and Computerizing Land Registration and Administration Systems*

Land administration systems in many SSA countries are characterized by time-consuming, inefficient, and expensive procedures for land transactions, a lack of transparency, corrupt practices, low public confidence in the systems, and generally insecure land transactions. A number of ways are available to address these inefficiencies and other problems in land administration, among them computerizing land registers and land administration systems. For example, according to the World Bank (2012), 27 economies worldwide that computerized their registries in the past seven years cut the average time to transfer property in half, by about three months. An increasing number of SSA countries have initiated programs to computerize land registers and establish LISs. While such interventions increase efficiency and transparency in land administration and facilitate movement of land from less to more productive users thereby raising returns for landholders, this is premised on the assumption that there is open and easy access to land registries. This is not the case for the vast majority of the rural landholders and land market participants especially in SSA (Deininger and Feder 2009). Therefore, measures to computerize land registration and administration systems must be accompanied by interventions to make the systems open and easily accessible to all stakeholders.

Programs for computerization and LIS development can take as long as 10 years to complete and require considerable financial resources and capacity building (McLaren 2011). For example, the first phase of the two-phase program of Uganda's LIS development has already absorbed US$11 million, with the second phase expected to absorb about US$10 million (see chapter 6). LISs are technologically and institutionally complex systems and include legally sensitive and economically important information, such as land titles and cadastral data; this requires building appropriate security measures to ensure data protection and system reliability.

The case study on Ghana and Uganda's LIS programs extracts a number of lessons and best practices, including the following:

- Establishing an LIS requires a systematic approach, a detailed system design, and careful planning of each phase.
- Design and implementation of the LIS and the associated activities are best done as a self-contained program or project within a wider land administration reform program, not as discrete activities of a project.
- An expert with global experience is required to act as a supervision engineer and adviser to supervise project implementation, similar to the practice in the building and construction industries.
- Free/Libre Open-Source Software versus commercial off-the-shelf software should be carefully chosen based on software maintenance, license payment, system security, and local capacity to keep the system operational.
- LIS development should be part not only of a broader reform agenda for the land sector but also of public services reform to ensure optimal impact.

Agricultural Land Redistribution and Land Administration in Sub-Saharan Africa
http://dx.doi.org/10.1596/978-1-4648-0188-4

### Managing and Inventorying of Government-Owned Land

State landownership is widespread in SSA. Many countries inherited legal provisions at independence that promoted the concept of public land, including unused customary land, which was readily used or simply claimed by governments. Countries with colonial white settlements nationalized many of the settlers' farm lands and corporate farms after independence. During the 1970s, others such as Benin, Burkina Faso, Nigeria, and Uganda either nationalized private and customary lands or established a state monopoly over land allocation, using this as a carte blanche to expand government landownership; this often created conditions for high levels of mismanagement and corruption (Mabogunje 1992). Improved governance of state-owned land has therefore become a challenge in many SSA countries.

Although auctioning state land for private sector development is one option, other efficient and equitable uses of state lands are available. For example, where state land has been occupied or used informally for a long time by private citizens, such as in rural and urban informal settlements or on agricultural land, long-term occupants could be legally recognized as owners and given land rights documents. Also, unoccupied or underused state land could be sold to land-poor farmers, as was done under a community-based land reform program in Malawi.

But to undertake any of these options, governments must first be able to identify and establish the ownership and occupancy status of state-owned lands. Currently, many SSA governments do not know the extent of their state landownership, because most lands are not surveyed and registered; in addition, they do not have up-to-date information on the current status of ownership and occupancy. To overcome this information gap and generate information for policy and decision making, some SSA governments have started inventorying state-owned land. The case study on government land inventories reviews Ghana and Uganda's experiences in identifying and registering their state-owned lands with a view to improving their management.

The case study finds that of the two countries, Ghana's program has been more successful, because it has been systematic and substantial, whereas Uganda's land inventory program is still recent and on a more limited scale. Ghana initiated its land inventory program in 2003 with two objectives: (1) to enable its land agencies to obtain up-to-date, accurate records on all government-acquired and -occupied lands and (2) to enable the government to formulate and implement policy guidelines on compulsory acquisitions, compensation, and divestiture of public lands no longer needed for their intended public purpose. The inventory program covered 722 out of an estimated 1,144 sites (63 percent). It provided a clearer picture of the composition of government land and the principal sources of tension in communities impacted by government land acquisitions. The findings of the program helped the government issue short-term policy guidelines for managing state land assets while waiting for results from the completed national inventory. Uganda's land inventory program was conducted from 2009 to 2011 and covered only 10 percent of its state lands. It faced design and implementation problems and was therefore cut short with a view to redesigning it for future implementation.

This case study's lessons and best practices indicate the following:

- Land inventory activities are best undertaken by specialized interdisciplinary teams of professionals drawn from the public and private sectors, with clearly defined responsibilities. Ghana's land inventory was executed by four teams of field officers, of which two were survey teams and two were valuation and land use planning teams.
- A sizable component of sensitization and training activities conducted by a carefully appointed interdisciplinary team of public and private sector professionals needs to be incorporated into the program.
- There should be public verification of a list of government-acquired and -occupied lands compiled from various sources before the list is finalized and used as a basis to contract out land inventories.
- In most typical settings, the private sector should undertake the field boundary survey, the collection of survey data, and the preparation of deed and survey plans, while the public sector should undertake quality assurance, approval of survey and deed plans, and title registration.

## Notes

1. *New African*, "South Africa 100 Years of Landless Blacks," September 18, 2013, http://www.newafricanmagazine.com/special-reports/other-reports/black-history-month/south-africa-100-years-of-landless-blacks.
2. A few exceptions of reasonably successful compulsory land reforms include those conducted in Japan, the Republic of Korea, and Taiwan, China, after the Second World War.
3. www.worldbank.org/lsms-isa.

## References

African Development Bank Group. 2010. *Agriculture Sector Strategy, 2010–2014*. Algiers: African Development Bank.

Ali, D., K. Deininger, and M. Goldstein. 2011. "Environmental and Gender Impacts of Land Tenure Regularization in Africa: Pilot Evidence from Rwanda." Policy Research Working Paper 5765, World Bank, Washington, DC.

Arial, A., C. Fagan, and W. Zimmermann. 2011. "Corruption in the Land Sector." IT Working Paper 04/2011, FAO and Transparency International, Berlin.

Bardhan, P., S. Bowles, and H. Gintis. 2000. "Wealth Inequality, Wealth Constraints and Economic Performance." In *Handbook of Income Distribution*, edited by A. B. Atkinson and F. Bourguignon, 549–603. North-Holland, Amsterdam.

Barraclough, S. L. 1970. "Agricultural Policy and Land Reform." *Journal of Political Economy* 78 (4): 906–47.

Barrett, C., M. F. Bellemare, and J. Y. Hou. 2010. "Reconsidering Conventional Explanations of the Inverse Productivity-Size Relationship." *World Development* 38 (1): 88–97.

Barrett, C. B. 1996. "On Price Risk and the Inverse Farm Size-Productivity Relationship." *Journal of Development Economics* 51 (2): 193–215.

Benjamin, D., and L. Brandt. 2002. "Property Rights, Labor Markets, and Efficiency in a Transition Economy: The Case of Rural China." *Canadian Journal of Economics* 35 (4): 689–716.

Berry, R. A., and W. R. Cline. 1979. *Agrarian Structure and Productivity in Developing Countries.* Baltimore, MD: Johns Hopkins University Press.

Binswanger, H. P., K. Deininger, and G. Feder. 1995. "Power, Distortions, Revolt and Reform in Agricultural Land Relations." In *Handbook of Development Economics,* edited by J. Behrman and T. N. Srinivasan, 2659–2772. Amsterdam: Elsevier Science.

Binswanger-Mkhize, H. P., C. Bourguignon, and R. J. E. van den Brink, eds. 2009. *Agricultural Land Redistribution: Toward Greater Consensus.* Washington, DC: World Bank.

Birdsall, N., and J. L. Londono. 1997. "Asset Inequality Matters: An Assessment of the World Bank's Approach to Poverty Reduction." *American Economic Review* 87 (2): 32–37.

Bruce, J. W., and A. Knox. 2009. "Structures and Stratagems: Decentralization of Authority over Land in Africa." *World Development* (Special Issue on the Limits of State-Led Land Reform) 37 (8): 1360–69.

Byamugisha, F. F. K. 2013. *Securing Africa's Land for Shared Prosperity: A Program to Scale Up Reforms and Investments.* Africa Development Forum Series. Washington, DC: World Bank.

Carletto, C., S. Savastano, and A. Zezza. 2013. "Fact or Artifact: The Impact of Measurement Errors on the Farm Size–Productivity Relationship." *Journal of Development Economics* 103: 254–61.

Collier, P., and S. Dercon. 2009. "African Agriculture in 50 Years: Smallholders in a Rapidly Changing World?" Paper presented at the Expert Meeting on "How to Feed the World in 2050," Food and Agriculture Organization of the United Nations Economic and Social Development Department, Rome, June 24–26.

Cotula, L., S. Vermeulen, R. Leonard, and J. Keeley. 2009. "Land Grab or Development Opportunity? Agricultural Investment and International Land Deals in Africa." IIED, FAO, and IFAD.

Deininger, K., D. A. Ali, S. Holden, and J. Zevenbergen. 2007. "Rural Land Certification in Ethiopia: Process, Initial Impact, and Implications for Other African Countries." Policy Research Working Paper 4218, World Bank, Washington, DC.

Deininger, K., D. Byerlee, J. Lindsay, A. Norton, H. Selod, and M. Stickler. 2011. *Rising Global Interest in Farmland: Can It Yield Sustainable and Equitable Benefits?* Washington, DC: World Bank.

Deininger, K., and G. Feder. 2009. "Land Registration, Governance and Development: Evidence and Implications for Policy." *World Bank Research Observer* 24 (2): 233–66.

Deininger, K., and L. Squire. 1998. "Economic Growth and Income Inequality: Reexamining the Links." *Finance and Development* 34 (1): 38–41.

Dinh, H. T., V. Palmade, V. Chandra, and F. Cossar. 2012. *Light Manufacturing in Africa: Targeted Policies to Enhance Private Investment and Create Jobs.* Washington, DC: World Bank.

Fafchamps, M., and J. Pender. 1997. "Precautionary Saving, Credit Constraints, and Irreversible Investment: Theory and Evidence from Semiarid India." *Journal of Business and Economic Statistics* 15 (2): 180–94.

Galor, O., and J. Zeira. 1993. "Income Distribution and Macroeconomics." *Review of Economic Studies* 60 (1): 35–52.

Hill, P. 1972. *Rural Hausa: A Village and a Setting.* Cambridge, U.K.: Cambridge University Press.

Jalan, J., and M. Ravallion. 1999. "Are the Poor Less Well Insured? Evidence on Vulnerability to Income Risk in Rural China." *Journal of Development Economics* 58 (1): 61–81.

Kevane, M. 1996. "Agrarian Structure and Agricultural Practice: Typology and Application to Western Sudan." *American Journal of Agricultural Economics* 78 (1): 236–45.

Kutcher, G. P., and P. L. Scandizzo. 1981. *The Agricultural Economy of Northeast Brazil.* Washington, DC: World Bank.

Larson, D. F., K. Otsuka, T. Matsumoto, and T. Kilic, 2012. "Should African Rural Development Strategies Depend on Smallholder Farms? An Exploration of the Inverse Productivity Relationship." Policy Research Working Paper 6190, World Bank, Washington, DC.

Mabogunje, A. L. 1992. "Perspectives on Urban Land and Urban Management Policies in Sub-Saharan Africa." Technical Paper 196, Africa Technical Department Series, World Bank, Washington, DC.

Mansuri, G., and V. Rao. 2012. *Localizing Development: Does Participation Work.* Policy Research Report. Washington DC: World Bank.

McLaren, R. A. 2011. "Module 12: ICT for Land Administration and Natural Resource Management." Draft Version 1.0–27/4/2011, Working Document, World Bank, Washington, DC.

Mookhrjee, D. 1997. "Informational Rents and Property Rights in Land." In *Property Relations, Incentives and Welfare*, edited by J. Romer, 3–39. New York: Macmillan.

Nolte, K. 2012. "Large Scale Agricultural Investments under Poor Land Governance Systems: Actors and Institutions in the Case of Zambia." Paper presented at the World Bank Annual Conference on Land and Poverty, Washington, DC, April 23–26.

Place, F. 2009. "Land Tenure and Agricultural Productivity in Africa: A Comparative Analysis of the Economics Literature and Recent Policy Strategies and Reforms." World Agroforestry Centre, Nairobi, Kenya.

Ribot, J. C. 2001. "Local Actors, Powers and Accountability in African Decentralization: A Review of Key Issues." Paper prepared for IDRC, Canada, Assessment of Social Policy Reforms Initiative, World Resources Institute, Washington, DC.

Sikor, T., and D. Muller. 2009. "The Limits of State-Led Land Reform: An Introduction." *World Development* (Special Issue on the Limits of State-Led Land Reform) 37 (8): 1307–16.

Simtowe, F., J. Mangisoni, and M. Mendola. 2011. *Independent Project Impact Evaluation of the Malawi Community-Based Rural Land Development Project.* First draft report, ITALTREND, Reggio Emilia, Italy.

Tanner, C. 2002. "Law Making in an African Context: The 1997 Mozambican Land Law." Food and Agriculture Organization of the United Nations Legal Papers Online 26. http://www.fao.org/fileadmin/user_upload/legal/docs/lpo26.pdf.

Torhonen, M. P., and D. Palmer. 2004. "Land Administration in Post-Conflict Cambodia." Paper presented at the Symposium on Post-Conflict Land Administration Areas, Geneva, Switzerland, April 29–30.

World Bank. 2004. "Malawi Community-Based Rural Land Development Project." Project appraisal document, World Bank, Washington, DC.

———. 2012. *Doing Business 2012: Doing Business in a More Transparent World.* Washington, DC: World Bank.

Zaibet, L. T., and E. G. Dunn. 1998. "Land Tenure, Farm Size, and Rural Market Participation in Developing Countries: The Case of the Tunisian Olive Sector." *Economic Development and Cultural Change* 46 (4): 831–48.

Zimmermann, W. 2002. "Comments on Land in Conflict and Post-Conflict Situations." Paper presented at the World Bank Land Workshop, Phnom Penh, June 4–6.

# CHAPTER 1

# Piloting Community-Based Land Reform in Malawi: Innovations and Emerging Good Practices

Hardwick Tchale

Land reforms and redistribution programs have been implemented in many countries to allocate land to the landless and land-poor segments of the population. Although generally consensus can be found on the need for land redistribution, often controversy abounds on how to do so peacefully and legally, without invoking rampant corruption, political interference, rent seeking, or social conflict (Binswanger-Mkhize, Bourguignon, and van den Brink 2009). A recent model that uses peaceful and legal means to transfer land is the community-based market-assisted approach piloted in Brazil in the 1990s and scaled up in recent years (World Bank 2009). Taking advantage of Brazil's experience, Malawi piloted the approach from 2004 to 2011. Malawi's experience offers constructive lessons, both good and bad, to other Sub-Saharan African (SSA) countries (World Bank 2004). This case study examines that experience to highlight the associated positive impacts accruing to beneficiaries in the form of productivity, income, and food security gains, and to draw important lessons for the design and implementation of similar interventions in other countries.

## Background

As in many other developing countries, land ownership in Malawi is highly skewed and the majority of the rights to access are insecure, because over 90 percent of Malawi's land is governed by customary regime. Although the usufruct rights under the customary system may be relatively secure, the rights are unregistered and not recognized under the statutory law. This poses challenges in terms of agricultural and rural development, given that over 80 percent of Malawi's population resides in rural areas and predominantly depends on agro-based livelihoods. As shown in table 1.1, 84 percent of all households and 94 percent of poor households depend on access to land for their livelihoods. As such, access to land therefore has a profound impact on food security and poverty reduction.

Although the challenges related to land access in Malawi are many and varied, the most significant one is the fragmentation of already small land parcels, which has led to extensive degradation. According to the 2008 Population Census, Malawi has an estimated population of 13.1 million and a total land area of 94,276 square kilometers (Government of Malawi 2008). Because of its small size, Malawi's population density is one of the highest in Africa. In 2008 average population density was estimated to be 139 persons per square kilometer. This average density masks important regional disparities: in the southern region, the average density reaches 185 persons per square kilometer, versus 154 in the central region and 63 in the north. Mounting population pressure has led to fragmentation, especially in the south where the pressure is the most intense. As shown in table 1.2, 76.9 percent of the households across Malawi have landholdings of less than 1 hectare, but the southern region is the most land-constrained, with landholding sizes of less than 0.5 hectares for nearly 60 percent of the households.

Another land challenge in Malawi relates to distributional issues. Table 1.2 shows the distribution of land under customary tenure. Over 16 percent of Malawi's population is landless, and the southern region has disproportionately more of the landless (18.7 percent). Ninety-five percent of the population holds

**Table 1.1  Households' Access to Land, by Type of Land, Region, and Poverty Status**
*percent*

|  | All land | | | Rain-fed | | | Dimba | | |
|---|---|---|---|---|---|---|---|---|---|
|  | *Nonpoor* | *Poor* | *Total* | *Nonpoor* | *Poor* | *Total* | *Nonpoor* | *Poor* | *Total* |
| North | 75 | 91 | 83 | 75 | 91 | 82 | 10 | 10 | 10 |
| Center | 82 | 93 | 86 | 82 | 93 | 86 | 14 | 17 | 15 |
| South | 69 | 95 | 81 | 69 | 95 | 81 | 7 | 9 | 8 |
| Total | 76 | 94 | 84 | 75 | 94 | 83 | 11 | 12 | 11 |

*Source:* Computed from the Integrated Household Survey collected by the National Statistical Office, 2010/11.
*Note: Dimba* is a local term for land, normally found in low-lying wetlands, usually with residual moisture, which is used for off-season (dry season) cultivation.

**Table 1.2  Distribution of Landholdings by Region, Poverty Status, and Wealth Quintiles**
*percent*

| Size (ha) | Total distribution | Total cumulative distribution | North | Center | South | Poor | Nonpoor | Wealth quintile | | | | |
|---|---|---|---|---|---|---|---|---|---|---|---|---|
|  |  |  |  |  |  |  |  | *1* | *2* | *3* | *4* | *5* |
| 0 | 16.4 | 16.4 | 17.4 | 13.5 | 18.7 | 6.2 | 24.4 | 4.9 | 6.4 | 9.2 | 15.0 | 36.7 |
| >0–0.2 | 3.0 | 19.4 | 1.9 | 1.4 | 4.6 | 3.0 | 2.9 | 2.5 | 3.7 | 2.8 | 3.0 | 2.8 |
| >0.2–0.5 | 29.3 | 48.7 | 23.9 | 23.2 | 36.1 | 35.1 | 24.9 | 37.8 | 33.6 | 32.0 | 26.3 | 21.7 |
| >0.5–1.0 | 28.2 | 76.9 | 29.9 | 30.5 | 25.8 | 33.5 | 24.1 | 32.9 | 34.9 | 31.0 | 28.5 | 18.6 |
| >1.0–2.0 | 18.2 | 95.1 | 21.9 | 24.5 | 11.6 | 18.6 | 17.8 | 18.7 | 18.0 | 19.4 | 21.2 | 14.6 |
| >2.0 | 4.9 | 100.0 | 4.9 | 6.8 | 3.3 | 3.7 | 5.9 | 3.2 | 3.4 | 5.5 | 6.0 | 5.7 |

*Source:* Computed from the Integrated Household Survey collected by the National Statistical Office, 2010/11.
*Note:* ha = hectares.

less than 2 hectares. Only 5 percent hold more than 2 hectares, and most of these are in the northern and central regions. In the leasehold tenure where government land is leased out, some studies allege significant land underutilization. For example, based on estimates from land utilization studies undertaken in Malawi more than a decade ago, 2.6 million hectares of suitable agricultural land remained uncultivated or underutilized in rural areas largely under leasehold (Government of Malawi 1997). In the midst of the growing land pressure, this implies that approximately 28 percent of Malawi's total land area has been lying idle or underutilized.[1] Malawi clearly needs nondistortionary policies and strategies that will improve land use efficiency by bringing this idle land into production. This could also help put more land into the hands of smallholders to make it more productive while improving smallholder incomes and contributing to agricultural development. Land is the most constraining factor to agricultural and rural development in Malawi. Discriminatory policies against agriculture, such as suppressed producer prices, export taxes on farm outputs, and overvalued exchange rates that encourage imports of primary products, have largely been eliminated.[2]

The government of Malawi realized that the land issues in the country required pragmatic solutions. Without instituting proper reforms, problems related to land pressure almost always degenerate into agrarian crisis. With this in mind, the government instituted the Presidential Commission on Land Reform in 1996. The commission was entrusted with the task of reviewing the previous land policy as well as the Land Act of 1965, which was essentially inherited from the colonial government. The commission's work culminated in the new land policy, adopted in 2002. In 2003 the government instituted a Special Law Commission to come up with a new land law on which to anchor the land policy. The new Land Bill was presented and passed by Parliament in 2013 but is yet to be assented to by the President. See table 1.3 for the chronology of land policy reforms in Malawi.

**Table 1.3  Chronology of Land Policy Reforms in Malawi**

| Date | Policy/act | Provisions |
|------|------------|------------|
| 1951 | The Land Ordinance | Defined land as either public, private, or customary, with the latter subsumed within public/crown land |
| 1965 | Land Act (Cap. 57:01) | Reinforced the Land Ordinance |
| 1967 | Registered Land Act (Cap. 58:01); Customary Development Act (Cap. 59:01); Local Land Boards Act (Cap. 60:01) | First comprehensive land law; incomplete application, marred by weak land administration capacity |
| 1996 | Presidential Commission on Land Policy Reform | The land policy recommendations contributed to the National Land Policy of 2002 |
| 2002 | National Land Policy | Recommended market-assisted land reform |
| 2003 | Special Law Commission | Review of the land law |
| 2004 | National Land Reform Program | Implementation strategy for the land policy |
| 2006 | Draft Land Bill | Legal framework for implementation of the new land policy; approval not granted, returned to Special Law Commission for review |
| 2013 | Draft Land Bill presented and passed in Parliament | Yet to be assented into law |

Agricultural Land Redistribution and Land Administration in Sub-Saharan Africa
http://dx.doi.org/10.1596/978-1-4648-0188-4

## Malawi's Community-Based Rural Land Development Pilot Project

To facilitate implementation of the new land policy, the government formulated the National Land Reform Program in 2004. Given the intricacies associated with implementation of land reforms, the government sought to undertake a pilot project to guide the implementation of the broader reform. This gave rise to the Community-Based Rural Land Development Project (CBRLDP).

Started in 2004, the CBRLDP piloted the implementation of a transparent, voluntary, legal, and resource-supported approach to land redistribution. The project initially included four districts (Machinga, Mangochi, Mulanje, and Thyolo), but was later extended to two additional districts (Balaka and Ntcheu) (see map 1.1 for the location of project sites). Its key design principles were to be market-assisted, community-driven, and focused on rural areas, where poverty was most pervasive. The pilot had three key elements: (1) voluntary acquisition by communities of land sold by willing estate owners; (2) resettlement and on-farm development, including transportation of settlers, establishment of shelter, and purchase of basic inputs and necessary advisory services; and (3) survey and registration of redistributed land. Land reform beneficiaries, organized in voluntary groups, were self-selected on the basis of predefined eligibility criteria. Each family received a grant of US$1,050, managed directly by beneficiaries, of which up to 30 percent was for land acquisition, and the rest for transportation, water, shelter, and farm development. Land for the project was acquired either from willing sellers, the government, or private donations and was registered initially under group title but with plans to issue individual titles upon demand in the future. Implementation was decentralized through District Assembly institutions and required capacity enhancement, especially for surveying and registration, using additional financing approved by the World Bank in 2009.

The project's development objective was to increase the agricultural productivity and incomes of about 15,000 poor rural families through the implementation of a decentralized, voluntary, community-based land redistribution project on eligible land in the project districts. In the additional financing phase of the project, the development objective was slightly modified, the outcome indicators were refined, and some new intermediate results were introduced in line with the modified activities, but the project remained largely the same in substance. The initial total project cost was about US$27.3 million, but the World Bank provided an additional US$10 million to assist the government with building its capacity in land administration. The project ended in September 2011.

## Assessment of Performance against Objectives and International Best Practices

The CBRLDP has been the most significant investment intervention implemented in postcolonial Malawi to address the highly unequal land ownership pattern. Overall, the CBRLDP has provided secure land to 15,142 poor rural families, enhancing their ability to build sustainable livelihoods.

**Map 1.1 Community-Based Rural Land Development Project Area Sites in Malawi**

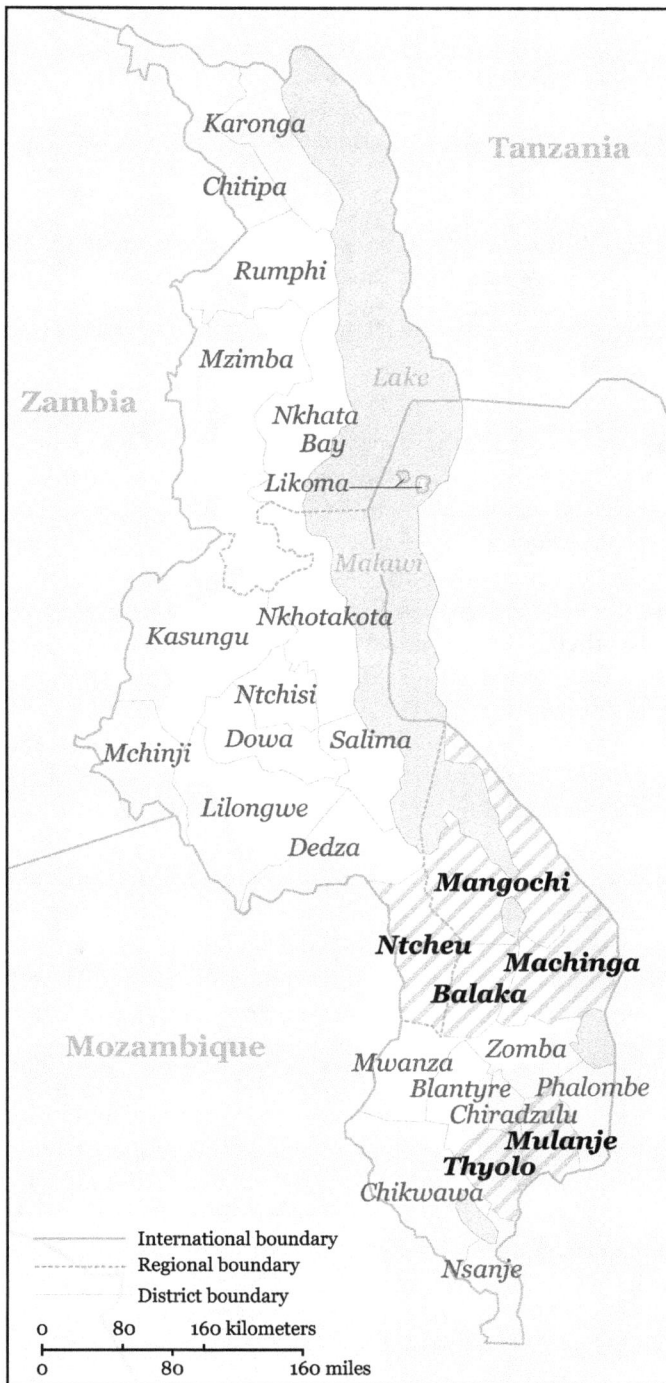

Karonga

Chitipa

Tanzania

Rumphi

Mzimba

Lake

Zambia

Nkhata Bay

Likoma

Malawi

Nkhotakota

Kasungu

Ntchisi

Mchinji

Dowa

Salima

Lilongwe

Dedza

**Mangochi**

**Ntcheu**

**Machinga**

**Balaka**

Mozambique

Mwanza

Zomba

Blantyre

Phalombe

Chiradzulu

**Mulanje**

**Thyolo**

Chikwawa

International boundary
Regional boundary
District boundary

Nsanje

| 0 | 80 | 160 kilometers |
| 0 | 80 | 160 miles |

*Source:* Machira 2009.

Agricultural Land Redistribution and Land Administration in Sub-Saharan Africa
http://dx.doi.org/10.1596/978-1-4648-0188-4

**Table 1.4  Summary of CBRLDP's Impacts (Selected Indicators)**

| Indicator | 2005/06 | 2006/07 | 2007/08 | 2008/09 |
|---|---|---|---|---|
| *Beneficiary households* | | | | |
| Landholding (ha) | 1.02 (0.93) | 1.81 (0.68) | 1.76 (0.69) | 1.79 (0.72) |
| Maize productivity (kg/ha) | 1,536 (1,176) | 2,476 (6,543) | 1,446 (1,200) | 1,464 (1,448) |
| Food security (months) | 6.16 (3.93) | 10.6 (3.21) | 8.53 (3.49) | 8.92 (3.55) |
| Agricultural income (Malawi kwacha) | 11,527 (38,914) | 31,141 (80,130) | 29,173 (57,347) | 44,683 (87,720) |
| *Nonbeneficiary households* | | | | |
| Landholding (ha) | 0.88 (0.62) | 0.92 (0.64) | 0.91 (0.69) | 0.95 (0.76) |
| Maize productivity (kg/ha) | 1,268 (995) | 1,309 (1,140) | 1,206 (885) | 1,474 (1,519) |
| Food security (months) | 7.74 (3.72) | 8.56 (3.79) | 7.44 (3.70) | 8.89 (3.70) |
| Agricultural income (Malawi kwacha) | 4,620 (18,291) | 6,089 (17,167) | 6,666 (22,627) | 10,616 (21,412) |

*Source:* Simtowe, Mangisoni, and Mendola 2011.
*Note:* CBRLDP = Community-Based Rural Land Development Project; ha = hectares; kg = kilograms.

Findings from a recent impact evaluation show that the project achieved most of its objectives (Simtowe, Mangisoni, and Mendola 2011). The actual number of beneficiaries relocated (15,142 households) exceeded the target of 15,000 households. Each of these households was given more than 1.5 hectares on average on which to cultivate various food and cash crops. Over 90 percent of the beneficiary groups also received title deeds for the land they acquired; hence their land tenure security was enhanced. The evaluation further indicated that, unlike other previous resettlement projects that were characterized by corruption, political interference, and violence, the CBRLDP's implementation process adhered to the selection criteria of beneficiaries stipulated in the project implementation plan. This led to peaceful resettlement and accelerated integration of the beneficiaries with the surrounding communities.

Land redistribution has led to significant positive impacts on the livelihoods of beneficiaries in surrounding as well as vacated communities. Participants reported improvements in landholdings, land tenure security, crop production, and productivity and consequently in income and food security (see table 1.4). Reports also demonstrate significant improvements in input use patterns for crop production (Simtowe, Mangisoni, and Mendola 2011).

The project also provided indirect benefits to surrounding communities through increased sources of cash income, increased food supply for purchase during the lean season, and increased populations for various development activities. Furthermore, beneficiaries' relatives in the vacated areas indirectly benefited through receipt of land left by beneficiaries and additional sources of cash income including remittances.

A financial and economic analysis conducted as part of the impact evaluation confirmed that the project was financially and economically viable: the financial and economic rates of returns were found to be high, with an economic rate of return of 20 percent (Simtowe, Mangisoni, and Mendola 2011).

## Emerging Innovative Aspects, Good Practices, and Lessons

Land can be acquired through various means, including grabbing, appropriation, compensation, and buying, depending on the tenure of the land in question. The government has vested powers within the current law to obtain land from anybody through a consultative process. In some cases though, compulsory land grabbing, mostly driven by strong political motives, has been justified on grounds of restitution. However, such approaches have invariably led to negative social and economic consequences. To avoid such adverse scenarios, the government of Malawi used a voluntary community-based, market-assisted, and willing seller–willing buyer approach. This was the most innovative aspect of the CBRLDP. It engendered voluntary participation (self-selection) for beneficiaries and landowners, and closely followed its core design and implementation principles (see box 1.1).

The design features and their meticulous implementation by the government led to the success of the project. Unlike many other land reform efforts, this project was implemented in an environment relatively free of the rampart corruption, rent seeking, and social conflicts documented elsewhere (Binswanger-Mkhize,

---

**Box 1.1  Core Design and Implementation Principles of the CBRLDP**

The key design and implementation features of the Community-Based Rural Land Development Project (CBRLDP) were chosen to ensure voluntary participation by beneficiaries and willingness to sell land by landowners, including acceptance by both the sending and receiving communities. The following are the core design and implementation principles:

- Land distribution will take place only on farm land acquired from willing sellers, on land transferred from government administration, or on land acquired through private donations.
- The project will explicitly exclude protected or fragile areas, or areas with restricted/limited agricultural potential.
- Beneficiaries will be self-selected, formed in groups on a voluntary basis, and subject to predefined eligibility criteria.
- Implementation will be decentralized through the existing District Assembly institutions, consistent with the Decentralization Policy.
- Project resources for land acquisition and farm development will be transferred directly to beneficiaries and will be managed by them.
- Land given to a beneficiary household should be sufficient to meet subsistence and economic viability.
- Beneficiaries will decide the property regime under which they will hold the land (i.e., leasehold, freehold, or customary estate).
- Enhanced capacity at all levels is a prerequisite for successful implementation of the project.
- Lessons learned from the pilot districts will determine the scope of future interventions.

*Source:* World Bank 2004.

---

Agricultural Land Redistribution and Land Administration in Sub-Saharan Africa
http://dx.doi.org/10.1596/978-1-4648-0188-4

Bourguignon, and van den Brink 2009) mainly because of the specific attention to the design details. A related innovative aspect was the use of Community Oversight Committees (COCs) in both the sending and receiving communities. COCs facilitated the identification of potential beneficiaries, assisted with all arrangements prior to departure, and facilitated the resettlement process, including the integration of beneficiaries in the receiving communities. The CBRLDP also played a critical role in strengthening the role of the Local Assembly and other local structures, which improved government ownership and commitment toward the project.

A final innovative aspect of the CBRLDP was its elaborate monitoring and evaluation (M&E) system, which, together with a functional management information system, provided timely feedback with which to make important decisions toward improving results. For example, providing beneficiaries with basic amenities such as water was introduced in response to feedback from periodic M&E reports. The M&E framework also incorporated the collection of panel data from the project's outset; these data have since been used to conduct an independent impact evaluation. This framework was meticulously implemented, thereby ensuring that important lessons can be drawn from the pilot to inform the design of subsequent land reform programs.

Overall, many aspects of the CBRLDP's design and implementation are considered best practice and an improvement over similar programs implemented earlier within Malawi and in other countries.[3] The CBRLDP is considered one of the best land redistribution programs implemented in SSA. Its design and implementation strategies have consistently shown results superior to those achieved with other means in other countries. As such, this case study highlights the key lessons drawn from the design and implementation of the CBRLDP:

- *Community-driven land reform programs are possible.* The CBRLDP demonstrated that with proper design, facilitation, and capacity building, community-driven land reform programs are possible and can be economically viable. In the pilot project, communities were able to self-select, engage landowners, and negotiate for land. All resources provided to facilitate the relocation process and the purchase of land were fully justified.

- *Beneficiaries prefer to relocate within or close to their original communities.* Although beneficiaries needed land, the majority preferred to relocate within or close to their original homes. A key disincentive to relocating is the need to preserve cultural and social ties; these are weakened when beneficiaries are relocated far away and/or across cultural and tribal lines. To reduce disputes that might arise from divergent cultural practices, the importance of sociocultural factors should not be underestimated.

- *The willing seller–willing buyer (WSWB) approach may not always work.* The market-assisted, WSWB approach, though comparatively better than other approaches, may not work in some cases. For example, in Thyolo and Mulanje districts, landowners were unwilling to sell their land to the government for purposes of resettlement under the project. In general, however, the approach minimizes political interference, corruption, and disputes, and as such it accelerates the peaceful integration of resettled households with receiving communities.

- *Institutional capacity is critical for successful implementation of such projects.* The CBRLDP's design assumed that estates had already been surveyed and therefore had established sizes and clear boundaries. However, this was not the case. Many leases were issued based on sketch plans, which did not match the actual plot sizes. Thus estates had to be resurveyed to confirm or establish their size and boundaries. This was a lengthy and costly exercise that negatively impacted the rate of transferring properties and processing new land titles for beneficiary groups. Thus there is a need to build capacity at all levels in land administration and management service delivery to ensure successful implementation of such programs.

- *A supportive policy and regulatory environment is essential.* Many of the institutional challenges faced by the CBRLDP were due to the lack of a supportive policy and legislative environment. Although the National Land Policy was adopted in 2002, the project was implemented in the absence of the new legal framework (the draft bill was tabled in Parliament in 2013 and is yet to be assented into law). To successfully scale up the land reform program in Malawi, the new Land Law is critical.

- *Land reform programs should be embedded within the broader rural development agenda.* One of the key challenges for the CBRLDP was the unanticipated need for other social amenities. Most beneficiaries were relocated into fairly remote areas with limited access to facilities (roads and transport services), inadequate schools, health facilities, and markets, and a lack of most other basic requirements, such as water. Although the project endeavored to provide safe water through the use of a farm development grant, provision of other amenities such as schools, health clinics, and other public services were beyond the scope of the project. It was expected that these amenities would be provided by the Local Development Fund, then implemented through the District Assemblies through the Malawi Social Action Fund.[4] However, the demand on local resources was overwhelming, and it was not possible for the CBRLDP to provide for all of the social needs of the newly relocated beneficiaries and the surrounding communities. As such, it is critical that projects like this be embedded within the broader rural development framework to ensure that beneficiaries are able to optimize the benefits from such programs.

## Notes

1. Given that this study was undertaken more than a decade ago, the situation could have changed given the increasing population (between 1998 and 2008, population grew by more than 30 percent).

2. Although up to now, in spite of the liberalized marketing policy, the government still continues to arbitrarily intervene in setting minimum prices for maize, tobacco, and cotton with potentially distortionary effects in the longer term.

3. For example, the Ndunda system implemented under the Lilongwe Rural Land Development Project, also funded by the World Bank during the 1970/80s.

4. The Local Development Fund (formerly the Malawi Social Action Fund) is a social development fund that has been supported by the World Bank through several phased projects dating back to the mid-1990s.

## References

Binswanger-Mkhize, H. P., C. Bourguignon, and R. van den Brink, eds. 2009. *Agricultural Land Re-distribution: Towards Greater Consensus*. Agriculture and Rural Development. Washington, DC: World Bank.

Government of Malawi. 1997. "Estate Land Utilization Study." Ministry of Lands and Valuation in Coordination with the UK Department for International Development, Lilongwe, Malawi.

———. 2008. *Population and Housing Census. Preliminary Report*. National Statistical Office, Zomba, Malawi.

Machira, S. 2009. "Pilot-Testing a Land Redistribution Program in Malawi." In Binswanger-Mkhize, H. P., C. Bourguignon, and R. van den Brink, eds. 2009. *Agricultural Land Re-distribution: Towards Greater Consensus*. Agricultural and Rural Development. Washington, DC: World Bank.

Simtowe, F., J. Mangisoni, and M. Mendola. 2011. *Independent Project Impact Evaluation of the Malawi Community-Based Rural Land Development Project*. First draft report, ITALTREND, Reggio Emilia, Italy.

World Bank. 2004. "Malawi Community-Based Rural Land Development." Project Appraisal Document, World Bank, Washington, DC.

———. 2009. *Brazil Land Based Poverty Alleviation 1*. Implementation Completion and Results Report, World Bank, Washington, DC.

# CHAPTER 2

# Land Redistribution in South Africa: A Critical Review

Edward Lahiff and Guo Li

Successful rural development and land reform are crucial for South Africa's economic and social future. As shown by international experiences in the past few decades, rural development is a strong force for spurring overall economic growth, reducing poverty, and enhancing food security (World Bank 2008). Having a vibrant and sustainable rural sector has also been proven vital for stimulating growth in other parts of the economy, particularly when a country is experiencing rapid urbanization. In South Africa, rural development and land reform carry additional strategic significance for achieving a higher degree of economic and social equity, creating more employment, and building stronger social cohesion—objectives that, to date, have largely not been achieved. It is not an exaggeration to claim that the success or failure in rural development and land reform will play a crucial role in determining the trajectory of South Africa's economic and social future.

This case study provides an overview of land reform in South Africa from 1994 to 2011. The focus is on South Africa's land redistribution program, but the study also touches briefly on restitution and tenure reform programs. The study begins with a brief sketch of South Africa's historical background before outlining the main aspects and achievements of its land reform programs to date. The final sections examine key challenges and new policy proposals facing land reform in South Africa.

## Origins and Patterns of Land Concentration

The extent to which the indigenous people of South Africa were dispossessed by European colonists—mainly Dutch and British settlers—was greater than in any other country in Africa, and it persisted for an exceptionally long time. European settlement began around the Cape of Good Hope in the 1650s and progressed northward and eastward over a period of 300 years. By the early 20th century, most of the country, encompassing most of the best agricultural land, was reserved for the minority white population, with the African majority confined to the Native Reserves (later, African Homelands or Bantustans), which constituted just 13 percent of the country. Beginning in the 1960s, the settler colonies of southern Africa strenuously resisted the decolonization of Africa, with the result that South Africa did not make the transition from the race-based system of apartheid to a democratic, nonracial government until 1994.

At the end of apartheid, approximately 82 million hectares of commercial farmland (86 percent of all farmland) were owned by the white minority (10.9 percent of the population), concentrated in the hands of approximately 60,000 owners.[1] More than 13 million black Africans, the majority of them poverty stricken, remained crowded onto the former homelands, where rights to land were generally unclear or contested. These areas were characterized by extremely low incomes and high rates of infant mortality, malnutrition, and illiteracy relative to the rest of the country. On private farms, millions of workers, former workers, and their families faced severe tenure insecurity and lack of basic facilities.

The transition from apartheid to democracy occurred through a negotiated settlement rather than an all-out war of liberation. This political compromise left intact much of the wealth and power of the white minority, including that over property rights. The new constitution—finalized in 1996—created the basis for a liberal democracy, albeit with an emphasis on socioeconomic rights and a clear mandate for the state to redress the injustices of the past. The constitutional clause on property guaranteed the rights of existing owners, but also granted specific rights of redress to victims of past dispossession and set the legal basis for a potentially far-reaching land reform program.

South African agriculture is of a highly dualistic nature, whereby a developed commercial sector coexists with large numbers of small farms on communal lands (NDA 2005; OECD 2006). The commercial sector generates substantial employment and export earnings,[2] but contributes relatively little to gross domestic product (GDP) in this highly urbanized and industrialized economy: Agriculture's share of GDP fell from 9.12 percent in 1965 to just 3.2 percent in 2002 (Vink and Kirsten 2003) and has fallen further since then. Although close to half of the South African population continues to reside in rural areas (Statistics South Africa 2006), most people are engaged in agriculture on a very small scale, if at all. They depend largely on nonagricultural income, including local wage employment and welfare grants, for their livelihoods, often migrating to cities to search for better opportunities.

## The Legal and Policy Basis for Land Reform

Land reform in South Africa seeks to address more than 350 years of race-based colonization and dispossession as part of the transition to a democratic society. Since 1994 South Africa has embarked on a multifaceted program of land reform designed to redress the racial imbalance in landholding and secure the land rights of historically disadvantaged people. Progress and impacts in all areas of the program are generally considered to have fallen far behind expectations and official targets.

The Constitution of the Republic of South Africa sets out the legal basis for land reform, particularly in its Bill of Rights, which places a clear responsibility on the state to carry out land and related reforms and grants specific rights to victims of past discrimination: "the public interest includes the nation's commitment to land reform, and to reforms to bring about equitable access to all South Africa's natural resources" (Constitution of the Republic of South Africa 1996, section 25, 4).[3] The constitution allows for expropriation of property for a public purpose or in the public interest, subject to just and equitable compensation.

The framework for land reform policy was set out in the "White Paper on South African Land Policy" in April 1997 (Government of South Africa, Department of Land Affairs 1997). Proposals to revise the White Paper were under discussion for many years and culminated in the release of a draft Green Paper in September 2011 (see the last section of this case study). Since 1994, land reform policy has been approached under three main areas:

- *Land restitution*, which provides relief for certain categories of victims of dispossession;
- *Tenure reform*, which intends to secure and extend the tenure rights of the victims of past discriminatory practices; and
- *Redistribution*, which focuses on acquiring land for certain categories of people through purchases on the open market.

The land reform program thus aims to achieve objectives of both equity (in terms of land access and ownership) and efficiency (in terms of improved land use), while also contributing to the development of the rural economy. These objectives, and the preferred means of achieving them, are described in the 1997 White Paper: "The purpose of the land redistribution program is to provide the poor with access to land for residential and productive uses, in order to improve their income and quality of life. The program aims to assist the poor, labor tenants, farm workers, women, as well as emergent farmers. Redistributive land reform will be largely based on willing-buyer willing-seller arrangements. Government will assist in the purchase of land, but will in general not be the buyer or owner" (Government of South Africa, Department of Land Affairs 1997, 38).

## Land Reform Programs and Their Implementation since 1994

### Land Restitution: Reclaiming Historical Rights

The legal basis for restitution was created under the Restitution of Land Rights Act (Act 22 of 1994), which provided for the restitution of historical land rights to people or communities dispossessed under racially based laws or practices after June 19, 1913. The Commission on Restitution of Land Rights was established under a chief land claims commissioner and seven regional commissioners. A special court, the Land Claims Court, with powers equivalent to those of the

High Court, was established to deal with land claims and other land-related matters. Legally, all restitution claims are against the state, rather than against past or current landowners; and provision is made for three broad categories of relief: restoration of the land under claim, granting of alternative land, or financial compensation.

The cutoff date for lodgment of restitution claims was December 31, 1998; the total number of claims lodged by then was 76,696, including individual (or family) and community claims. More than 60,000 of the claims lodged related to urban land: all were settled by 2009, the great majority by means of cash compensation, although there were some notable land restorations, such as the District Six area in Cape Town. Rural land claims, many of which involve large communities claiming extensive properties from both private and public owners, have proven to be particularly difficult and costly to settle, specifically those involving the forestry and mining sectors. According to figures obtained by the Institute for Poverty, Land and Agrarian Studies (May 2011), a total of 10,274 rural claims had been settled by the end of March 2011.[4] In 2010 the Department of Rural Development and Land Reform (DRDLR) reported a total of 4,560 outstanding land claims; since then, at least 457 have been settled, leaving about 4,000 outstanding claims, all of which appear to be rural (DRDLR 2011).

Given the large areas of often high-value agricultural land restored to communities under the restitution program, and widespread reports of underutilization of land or collapses in agricultural production, various attempts have been made to involve private-sector commercial partners in restitution projects, usually referred to as "strategic partnerships," with mixed results (Derman, Lahiff, and Sjaastad 2006; Lahiff, Davis, and Manenzhe 2012). Since 2010 numerous restitution cases have been included in the DRDLR's "Recapitalization and Development Program," whereby public funds have been used either to provide on-farm infrastructure or to finance commercial partnerships.

### Tenure Reform: Securing Land Rights

Tenure reform in rural South Africa refers both to the protection and strengthening of the rights of occupiers of privately owned farms and state land (for example, farm workers and tenants) and to the reform of the system of communal tenure prevailing in the former homelands.

Almost all land in the rural areas of the former homelands is legally owned by the state, in trust for particular communities. These areas are characterized by severe overcrowding and numerous unresolved disputes in which the rights of one group of land users overlap with those of another. Today the administration of communal land is spread across a range of institutions, such as tribal authorities (traditional councils) and provincial departments of agriculture, but it is almost dysfunctional in many areas. For example, there is widespread uncertainty about the validity of documents (e.g., permission-to-occupy certificates), the appropriate procedures for transferring land within families, and the legality of leasing or selling rights to land (Ntsebeza 2006; Cousins 2007).

Initial attempts to draft a law for the comprehensive reform of land rights and administration in communal areas were abandoned in mid-1999 in the face of stiff opposition from traditional leaders. A revised Communal Land Rights Act (CLaRA) was passed by Parliament in 2004. The CLaRA was intended to give secure land tenure rights to communities and individuals who occupy and use land previously reserved for occupation by African people and registered in the name of the state or held in trust (Government of South Africa, Department of Land Affairs 2004). Although supported by the traditional chiefs, these measures were criticized by a range of trade unions, women's organizations, the South African Human Rights Commission, and land rights nongovernmental organizations (NGOs) as perpetuating the undemocratic rule of tribal chiefs and failing to secure the rights of individuals, especially women (Walker 2003; Claassens and Cousins 2008). In May 2010, following legal challenges from four rural communities, the Constitutional Court declared the CLaRA unconstitutional. A 15-year search for tenure reform in the country's communal areas effectively came to a halt.

The Extension of Security of Tenure Act of 1997 (ESTA) was intended to provide protection from illegal eviction for people who live on rural or peri-urban land with the permission of the owner, regardless of whether they are employed by the owner. Although the ESTA makes it more difficult to evict occupiers, evictions within the law are possible, and illegal evictions remain common. A study by Wegerif, Russell, and Grundling (2005) found that more than 2 million farm dwellers—many of them tenant farmers engaged in independent production—were displaced between 1994 and 2004, greater than the number displaced in the last decade of apartheid (1984–94) and more than the total number who had benefited under all aspects of the official land reform program since it began.[5] In theory, ESTA allows farm dwellers to apply for grants for on- or off-farm developments (for example, housing) and gives the Minister of Land Affairs the power to expropriate land for such developments, but neither of those measures has been used widely to date (Cousins and Hall 2011). Where grants have been provided, they have usually involved farm residents moving off farms and into townships, rather than granting them agricultural land of their own or securing them accommodation on farms where they work.[6]

One category of farm dwellers—labor tenants—was expected to acquire much stronger legal rights. The term "labor tenant" refers to black tenants on white-owned farms who pay for their use of agricultural land through the provision of labor as opposed to cash rental. The Land Reform (Labor Tenants) Act of 1996 protects labor tenants from eviction and gives them the right to acquire ownership of the land that they live on or use. Approximately 19,000 claims have been lodged under the act, mostly in the provinces of KwaZulu-Natal and Mpumalanga; only a minority of those claims have been settled to date. Indeed, virtually no specific mention is made of labor tenants in recent government documents (i.e., DRDLR reports for 2009/10 or 2010/11). Neither the Labor Tenants Act nor ESTA has succeeded in meeting its chief objectives of preventing illegal evictions and securing land rights—failures that can be attributed largely to a lack of dedicated budgets for tenure reform on the part of the Department of Land Affairs (DLA) and a lack of enforcement of the law by police, prosecutors, and the courts (Hall 2003; Xaba 2004; Human Rights Watch 2011). A Farm Workers' Summit held in Cape Town in July 2010 highlighted the continuing problems of poor pay and conditions and widespread mistreatment of farmer workers and farm dwellers.

In February 2010, *Business Day* reported that less than 2 percent of redistributed land had gone to farm workers (including labor tenants), although it is likely that some labor tenants were included in projects without being specifically mentioned.[7] Commitments by successive government ministers to reform both ESTA and the Labor Tenants Act were advanced somewhat by the publication of the draft Tenure Security Bill in December 2010, which would replace existing legislation in this area of farm dwellers' rights, but these proposals have yet to be passed into law.

### Redistribution: Shifting the Balance of Landholding and Production

Whereas restitution and tenure reform programs cater to specific groups of people who have legally enforceable rights (programs generally referred to as "rights based"), redistribution is a more discretionary program that seeks to redress the racial imbalance in rural landholding on a more substantial scale. The legal basis for redistribution is the 1998 Provision of Land and Assistance Act (formally known as the Provision of Certain Land for Settlement Act of 1993), but this is no more than an enabling act that empowers the Minister of Land Affairs to provide funds for land purchase. The details of the redistribution program are thus contained in various policy documents and official statements rather than in legislation. The methods chosen by the state to bring about redistribution are mainly, although not entirely, based on the operation of the land market, but this is not a strict constitutional requirement. Redistribution policy has undergone a series of changes since 1994, with gradual shifts from a focus on poorer beneficiaries to the somewhat better-off, and from a relatively passive to a more proactive role for the state in land purchases.

The defining feature of South Africa's redistribution policy to date—and the one that has been most controversial—has been the reliance on voluntary purchase of land at market prices, a policy widely referred to as "willing seller–willing buyer" (WSWB). The concept of WSWB gradually entered the discourse around land reform in South Africa during the period 1993–96, reflecting the shift in economic thinking within the African National Congress (ANC)—the dominant party within the liberation movement—from left-nationalist to neoliberal (Lahiff 2007). The principle was absent entirely from the ANC's "Ready to Govern" policy statement of 1992, which instead advocated expropriation and other non-market mechanisms, and from the Reconstruction and Development Program, the manifesto on which the party came to power in 1994. An extensive program of consultation by the newly created DLA, both within the country and with international advisers, led to a new policy direction, outlined in the 1997 White Paper on South African Land Policy, which made a market-based approach—and particularly the WSWB concept—the cornerstone of land reform policy (World Bank 1994; Williams 1996; Government of South Africa, Department of Land Affairs 1997; Hall, Jacobs, and Lahiff 2003). Such an approach was not dictated by the South African constitution but can be seen as a policy choice in line with emerging international trends and with the macroeconomic strategy (the Growth, Employment, and Redistribution Strategy) adopted by the ANC in 1996.

Until 2000 redistribution policy centered on provision of the Settlement/ Land Acquisition Grant (SLAG—later renamed the Settlement/Production Land Acquisition Grant [SPLAG]), a grant of R 16,000 to qualifying households with an income of less than R 1,500 a month. This phase of redistribution generally was described as targeting the "poorest of the poor," which appears to have been done with some success. However, it also was criticized widely for "dumping" large groups of poor people on former commercial farms without the skills or resources necessary to bring them into production. After 2001, SLAG was largely replaced by the Land Redistribution for Agricultural Development (LRAD) program, which was introduced with the explicit aim of promoting commercially oriented agriculture, but claimed to cater to other groups as well. LRAD offered higher grants, paid to individuals rather than to households, and made greater use of loan financing through institutions such as the state-owned Land Bank to supplement the grant. All beneficiaries were expected to make a contribution, in cash or kind, the size of which determined the value of the grant for which they qualified. In a minority of cases, groups of farm workers used grants (either SLAG or LRAD) to purchase equity shares in existing farming enterprises, especially in areas of high-value agricultural land, such as the fruit-growing and wine-producing lands of the Western Cape. Share-equity schemes have been criticized for perpetuating highly unequal relationships between white owner-managers and black worker-shareholders, and for providing few material benefits to workers (Mayson 2003; Kleinbooi, Lahiff, and Boyce 2006; Human Rights Watch 2011, 78). The farm equity program was suspended in 2009 but relaunched in 2011 in response to pressures from the government of the Western Cape Province.

Under both SLAG and LRAD, grants were issued to specific individuals who were then responsible for sourcing and negotiating the purchase of land from private owners. Since 2006, however, these grant-based programs have been overshadowed by the new Proactive Land Acquisition Strategy (PLAS). Under this approach, the state buys land directly from owners, without necessarily identifying intended beneficiaries in advance. This state-owned land is subsequently allocated to approved beneficiaries on a leasehold basis for three to five years, following which the lessee may be allowed an option to purchase.

### Achievements to Date

Land reform in South Africa has consistently fallen far behind the targets set by the state and behind popular expectations. In 1994 virtually all commercial farmland in the country was controlled by the white minority, and the incoming ANC government set a target for the entire land reform program (restitution,

**Table 2.1  Total Land Transfers under South Africa's Land Reform Programs, 1994–2011**

| Program | Number of hectares transferred | Total transferred (%) |
|---|---|---|
| Redistribution | 3,447,228 | 55.53 |
| Restitution | 2,760,527 | 44.47 |
| Total | 6,207,755 | 100.00 |

Source: *Umhlaba Wethu* 13, June 2011. http://www.plaas.org.za/sites/default/files/publications-pdf/UW %2013.pdf.

tenure reform, and redistribution) to transfer 30 percent of white-owned agricultural land within a five-year period (ANC 1994). The target period was subsequently extended to 20 years (that is, to 2014), and in November 2009, the Director General of DRDLR suggested extending the deadline to 2025. The fact is that, in recent years, senior policy makers played down the importance of a particular timescale or percentage-based target, choosing instead to focus on a qualitative target of "deracialization and productive use."

The government has tended to attribute this slow progress to resistance from landowners and to the high prices demanded for land,[8] but independent studies point to a wider range of factors, including complex application procedures and bureaucratic inefficiency (Hall 2004a). Major budgetary shortfalls in the area of restitution from 2008 to 2010 and growing concerns around the collapse of production on land acquired under both restitution and redistribution have shifted policy away from land acquisition toward the productive use of land.

By March 2011, it was estimated that a total of 6.27 million hectares of land had been transferred to beneficiaries under the entire land reform program; of this, approximately 55 percent was transferred under the redistribution program (including tenure reform and commonage) and the remaining 45 percent under the restitution program (see table 2.1). As with other areas of the land reform program, however, detailed statistics on beneficiaries, the geographical spread of projects, the type of land acquired, and the types of financing used are generally unavailable.

The total land area transferred is equivalent to 7.2 percent of the agricultural land under white ownership in 1994, although some of this has actually come from land previously owned by the state. To this can be added sizable areas transferred through private market transactions; on the downside, large numbers of farm dwellers (workers, tenants, and their dependents) have lost access to land on white-owned commercial farms since 1994.

## Key Policy Issues in South Africa's Land Reform Program

This section examines some of the key challenges facing South Africa's land reform program, particularly in the area of land redistribution, drawing on a range of official documents, qualitative case studies, and gray literature. It also discusses some recent policy developments.

### Land Acquisition

The manner in which land is to be selected, acquired, and paid for has been the most contentious issue in South African land reform policy since 1994. This contrasts with the relatively little attention given to issues such as beneficiary selection or land use. The WSWB approach that defines the redistribution model in South Africa was based on the World Bank's recommendations for a market-led reform, emphasizing the voluntary nature of the process; payment of full market-related prices, up front and in cash; a reduced role for the state (relative to previous "state-led" reforms elsewhere in the world); and the removal of various "distortions" within the land market (World Bank 1994). The WSWB approach also fits well with the general spirit of reconciliation and compromise that characterized the negotiated transition to democracy, although it goes considerably farther than the requirements of the 1996 constitution. The South African approach to redistribution diverges, however, from the model promoted by the World Bank in several important respects, particularly in its failure to introduce a land tax to discourage speculation and dampen land prices, the effective avoidance of expropriation (even when dealing with difficult cases), its failure (up until very recently) to allow beneficiaries to design and implement their own projects, and its failure to promote subdivision of large holdings.

The WSWB approach has remained at the center of the South African land reform despite widespread opposition and recurring promises of "review" from government leaders. At the National Land Summit in July 2005, for example, abandonment of that approach was the uppermost demand from civil society and landless people's organizations, and it was the subject of criticism by both the state president and the Minister of Land Affairs at the time. Representatives of large-scale landowners remain broadly in favor of the approach, especially the payment of market-related prices, although they have been critical of protracted processes around land purchase and payment (Lahiff 2007). Since 2005 repeated reference has been made to "reviews" of WSWB (ongoing or planned) by the departments concerned (see DRDLR 2009) by the state president, and by successive Ministers for Land Affairs and Rural Development and Land Reform. In June 2009, for example, Minister Nkwinti told Parliament that the government would scrap the WSWB system, which was too expensive and too slow in transferring land to black people.[9]

Using the market as a means of acquiring land for redistribution has obvious attractions in South Africa, especially where land purchases are to be funded entirely or largely by the state. South Africa has an active land market and a well-developed market infrastructure, which undoubtedly presents many opportunities for land acquisition. The weaknesses that have become apparent in the WSWB approach are largely in three areas: the suitability of land being offered for sale, the prices being demanded, and bureaucratic delays (exacerbated by budgetary shortfalls) in funding purchases.

The market-led approach as implemented in South Africa offers landowners absolute discretion in deciding whether to sell their land, to whom they will sell it, and at what price, with the result that most land that comes onto the market is not offered for land reform. Many landowners are politically opposed to land reform or they lack confidence in the process, especially the slow process of negotiation and payment. If possible, they prefer to sell their land to other buyers. Reports suggesting that land being offered for land reform purposes is of inferior quality have been widespread (Lyne and Darroch 2003; Tilley 2004). In addition, complaints—from land reform beneficiaries, officials, and politicians—repeatedly claim that where land is offered, excessive prices are being demanded (Government of South Africa, Department of Land Affairs 2005). Indeed, the high prices being paid for land have been a recurring cause for complaint in successive reports from the DRDLR, but with little reflection on failures of the state to use its available powers to secure better terms.

Land price information for the first decade of the land reform program (1994–2004) shows that average prices paid for land under both the redistribution and the restitution programs have diverged considerably from the pattern for the general market (see figure 2.1). With the exception of two years within this period (1995 and 1996), prices paid for land under the redistribution program have been below those of the general land market—by an average of 33 percent since 1997. By contrast, prices paid for land under the restitution program, having remained below market prices for the period 1994–99, have exceeded market prices every year since 2000, reaching 2.5 times the general market price in 2004. Repeated complaints by senior policy makers suggest that this trend has continued beyond 2004, as land reform payouts continue to run

**Figure 2.1  Prices for Land under Redistribution and Restitution Programs versus Market Prices (1994–2004)**

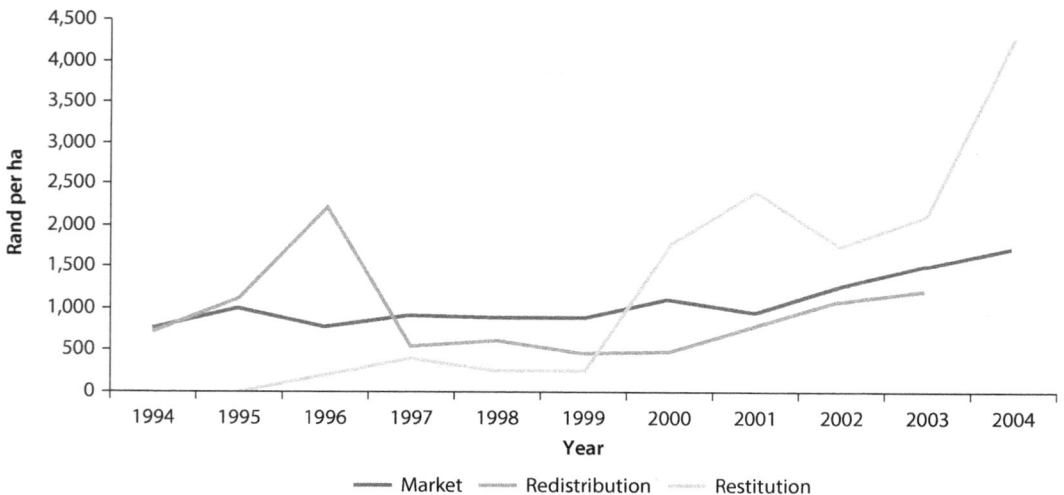

*Source:* Unpublished data from a draft report prepared by the Government of South Africa's DLA, the World Bank, and the Human Sciences Research Council, 2007.
*Note:* ha = hectares.

far ahead of expectations and of budgets, but whether prices paid exceed market norms remains to be tested.

Criticisms of the market-based approach that underpins WSWB center on the slow pace of land transfer, a widespread belief (inside and outside government) that landowners are receiving a price premium, and a strong political sentiment—especially from the left-wing of the liberation movement—that white landowners should not be rewarded for land that was taken from black people by force (see Ntsebeza 2007).

The most important change in the area of land acquisition since 1994 was the adoption of the PLAS policy in 2005–06. Emerging in the context of widespread public concern about the pace of land transfer and the high prices being paid for land, PLAS offered a more direct role for the state in identifying and acquiring land on behalf of potential beneficiaries. Provincial-level officials could now negotiate purchases directly with willing local landowners on the basis of official estimates of land needs in an area. Potential beneficiaries, who were previously responsible for identification of land and initial negotiations with landowners, now play little role in the process—indeed, the selection of land and price negotiations are generally completed before specific beneficiaries are even identified.

Since its inception, PLAS has become the biggest single redistribution program in terms of both budget and land area. For example, land acquired under PLAS accounted for 49 percent of total land area in 2007/08 and rose to 85.6 percent in 2010/11 (Government of South Africa, Department of Land Affairs 2008; DRDLR 2011). Under PLAS, land is registered in the name of the state and provided to approved beneficiaries by means of lease or caretakership agreements, typically of three or five years' duration (DRDLR 2009). After this period, the land may be transferred permanently to beneficiaries in terms of an LRAD, SPLAG, or Commonage Grant, subject to official approval. It is unclear from official reports how much of the land acquired proactively has actually been allocated to beneficiaries or how many leaseholders have gone on to become owners.[10]

As with previous policies, the supply of land and the price to be paid is entirely at the discretion of landowners, and there is no indication that landowners have been put under any pressure either to make land available or to compromise on price. Moreover, implicit in PLAS is the requirement that landowners are willing to participate in often-protracted processes with state officials, rather than disposing of their land through more conventional market channels. There would appear to be incentives for landowners to offer land that they might otherwise have difficulty disposing of through other channels, or to expect to receive a premium price. Under such conditions, the prices paid for land are likely to reflect the (often unequal) negotiating skill of (private) sellers and (public) buyers.

The "proactive" purchase of land—presented as a means of accelerating land acquisition—has also brought about a little-acknowledged shift from a demand-driven process (albeit a poorly performing one) to a largely supply-driven one. Land officials, eager to spend their budgets and meet their targets, and without specific beneficiaries to satisfy, now enjoy wide discretion in the selection of land and are likely to be influenced (in terms of both choice and price of land) by landowners' willingness to sell. There is no indication, however, that higher volumes, better quality, or lower prices have been achieved as a result of this policy shift.

### Beneficiary Targeting

From the beginning, the intended beneficiaries of South Africa's land reform program have been defined in very broad, and almost exclusively racial, terms. The 1997 White Paper included the poor, labor tenants, farm workers, women, and emergent farmers, but no specific strategies or system of priorities were developed to ensure that such groups actually benefit. As in other areas of land reform, a critical shortage of data exists, from government or independent sources, leading to much speculation on the socioeconomic profile of beneficiaries, especially since the introduction of LRAD in 2001. The limited evidence, however, would suggest that young people, the unemployed, and farm workers have been served particularly poorly.

Because the redistribution program has been based largely on beneficiaries' self-selection, effectively no targeting is seen of applicants in terms of income or agricultural experience.[11] Under SLAG (from 1995 to 2000), a household income ceiling of R 1,500 per month was set (but not always enforced). However, the low level of the grant and the requirement that people acquire land in groups (often comprising more than 100 people) were probably effective in targeting relatively poor people and deterring the better-off.

DLA's Quality of Life Survey, conducted in 1999, found that 75 percent of beneficiaries fell below the poverty line, levels of participation by female-headed households were high (31 percent nationally), and more than 20 percent of household heads were unemployed (May and Roberts 2000, 12). The 2002 Quality of Life Survey supported the earlier survey's findings that land reform was successfully targeting the poorer sections of rural society (Ahmed et al. 2003, 196).

The switch to LRAD in 2001, however, with its larger grant sizes and its emphasis on more commercial forms of production, undoubtedly shifted the emphasis toward small groups (often family based) of better-off applicants— although again the data are extremely sparse. This change, and the emphasis on relatively large-scale commercial farming (in the absence of subdivision), also shifted land reform toward a simple deracialization of commercial agriculture rather than the radical restructuring that had been envisioned by many people in the land sector in the early years of the program. The greater emphasis now paid to economic "viability" was also in line with an emerging policy direction centering on black economic empowerment (BEE), which emphasized the participation of black people in all sectors of the economy.

Over time, the trend has shifted toward targeting individuals considered more likely to be successful farmers. According the Director General of DRDLR, the policy of the department is "[T]o ensure our redistributed and restituted land goes only to people who can make optimal use of it" (DRDLR 2009). To achieve this objective, the department developed a strategy that includes the selection and categorization of land reform beneficiaries into five groups: landless households, commercially ready subsistence producers, expanding commercial smallholders, well-established black commercial farmers, and financially capable aspirant farmers. According to the DRDLR, this will help in the appropriate design of land reform products and support services.

The Quality of Life surveys employed during the early years of the land reform were not continued through this period, and official information on the socioeconomic profile of beneficiaries is virtually nonexistent. The growing emphasis on effective use of redistributed land over the past decade, and the limited evidence of any effective provision for the poor (as described above), means that by 2011, beneficiary selection was decreasingly on the basis of need and increasingly on the basis of ability to use land productively. Ongoing problems with underutilization of land and the collapse of production in many land reform areas indicate, however, that shifts in beneficiary targeting have not been sufficient to overcome the deep problems being encountered by newly resettled farmers, as discussed below.

### Farm Planning and Land Use

Land reform in South Africa to date has involved the transfer of relatively large commercial farms in their entirety to groups of beneficiaries. The country's large commercial farming units—typically in the range of 100–1,000 hectares—arose historically from a combination of ecological and political factors, including forced dispossession of black occupiers, generous state subsidies to white owners under apartheid, and various forms of forced (and thus cheap) labor. Many would-be beneficiaries of land reform undoubtedly would prefer to gain access to relatively small areas of land on a household basis, but more often than not they have found themselves owning large farms as part of a sizable collective. In many cases, such groups have attempted to operate farms on a collective basis (i.e., as a single farming operation), whereas in others they have implemented a degree of informal subdivision, particularly for cultivated lands. Shared grazing may also be used by owners of individual herds, but such individualization of production does not usually receive the support of state agencies such as the national DRDLR or provincial departments of agriculture. Under LRAD, there was a move toward smaller groups, including extended family groups, because of the increased availability of finance in the forms of grants and credit (van den Brink, Thomas, and Binswanger 2007). In addition, removing the income ceiling for grants facilitated entrance into the redistribution program of black businesspeople who are able to engage more effectively with officials and landowners to design projects and obtain parcels of land that match their needs.

The prevalence of group "projects" has been driven by a combination of the small size of the available grant relative to the cost of the typical agricultural holding, which has forced beneficiaries to pool their grants, and a virtual ban on the subdivision of large-scale commercial farms. Official opposition to subdivision of farms has deep roots in South African history, and it has been a persistent feature of land reform since 1994.[12] The failure to subdivide is arguably the single greatest contributor to the failure and general underperformance of land reform projects because it not only foists inappropriate farm sizes on people (and absorbs too much of their grants in the process, leaving little over for production), but also forces them to work in groups, whether they want to or not.[13] The World Bank has long argued for subdivision, but its position has been consistently opposed by most of the South African agricultural "establishment."

It is difficult to explain this failure to contemplate subdivision, and the topic has rarely been debated, but a number of factors may contribute to this phenomenon. Group acquisition has not been openly questioned by organizations representing the landless, perhaps in the belief that beneficiaries will feel better in a mutually supportive group. The limited evidence from existing land reform projects, however, suggests that large groups do not translate into effective production units or into benefits for members;[14] and many groups collapse into individual production, usually at a very low level of output and with little tenure security for such individuals. The collective ("community") basis of many restitution claims and the requirement that people organize themselves into groups to access grants under the redistribution program have also contributed to the prevalence of collective landholding and attempts at collective production. This progression from applying for land as a group to using land collectively was not inevitable, however, especially if beneficiaries were to be given (or insisted upon getting) greater freedom of choice.

The most immediate explanation for the lack of subdivision remains the requirement imposed by officials of the DRDLR, provincial departments of agriculture, and the regional land claims commissioners that, as a condition of grants and settlement awards, groups implement "whole farm" plans that conform to the imagined norms of large-scale commercial farming. In this requirement, the state is supported by the vast majority of agricultural economists and commercial farmers in the country who are clearly hostile to a radical restructuring of the existing commercial agricultural sector based on large farms. If, however, the state had a policy of systematically breaking up large farms into smaller units suitable for emerging farmers—whether organized as households or in small groups—a very different outcome might be possible.

Retaining former commercial farms as undivided properties, however, is only one aspect of the farm model being imposed as part of the South African land reform. In many other ways as well, groups of generally resource-poor, risk-averse, and inexperienced black farmers are required to conform to the imagined ideal of an individual commercial farmer. This demand starts with the "business plan" typically drawn up by consultants or officials of the Department of Agriculture who have been exposed only to large-scale commercial farming and that relate almost entirely to the physical properties of the land, rather than to the socioeconomic characteristics or the expressed wishes of the new owner-occupiers. Market production is usually the only objective, and business plans typically require substantial loans from commercial banks, purchases of heavy equipment, selection of crop varieties and livestock breeds previously unknown to the beneficiaries, hiring of labor (despite typically high rates of unemployment among members themselves), and often the appointment of a full-time farm manager. Not surprisingly, much of that typically fails to materialize.

Thus a defining characteristic of South African land reform policy is that beneficiaries—no matter how poor or how numerous—are required to step into the shoes of former white owners and continue to manage the farm as a unitary, commercially oriented enterprise; in other words, beneficiaries must adapt to the needs of the ideological paradigm of "big commercial farms," not the other way around. Alternative models, based on low material inputs, high labor inputs, and smaller units or even household-based production, are actively discouraged. The failure to provide land reform beneficiaries with appropriately sized farms, and the resulting tensions within many beneficiary groups, are undoubtedly a major contributor to the high failure rate of land reform projects.

### Postsettlement Support

In terms of market-led land reform, beneficiaries should not rely exclusively on the state for postsettlement support services, but should be able to access services from a range of public and private providers. Indeed, the past two decades have seen a major reduction in the overall state services available to farmers. Whereas large commercial farmers have generally managed to overcome this service decline through their access to a range of commercial and cooperative services, land reform beneficiaries and other small-scale farmers are largely left to fend for themselves (Vink and Kirsten 2003). Numerous studies—supported by statements from senior policy makers—reveal that land reform beneficiaries experience numerous problems accessing services, such as credit, training, technology extension, and transport as well as plowing, veterinary, and marketing services (HSRC 2003; Hall 2004b; Wegerif 2004; Bradstock 2005).

Services available to land reform beneficiaries tend to be supplied by provincial departments of agriculture and a small number of NGOs, but the evidence suggests that these reach only a minority of projects. In a study of LRAD projects in three provinces, for example, the Human Sciences Research Council reports that "in many cases there is still no institutionalized alternative to laying the whole burden of training, mentoring and general capacitation on the provincial agricultural departments" (HSRC 2003, 72). In a study of nine LRAD projects in the Eastern Cape Province, Hall (2004b) finds that not one had obtained any support from the private sector and most had not had any contact with the DLA since obtaining their land; two had received infrastructure grants from the Department of Agriculture, but none were receiving any form of extension service. In November 2005, the Minister for Agriculture and Land Affairs told Parliament that 70 percent of land reform projects in Limpopo Province were dysfunctional, a situation she attributed to poor design, negative dynamics within groups, and a lack of postsettlement support.[15] In 2010–11, 411 farms were reported to have been provided with "functional agricultural infrastructure" under the Recapitalization and Development Program, a tiny proportion of the number acquired since 1994 (DRDLR 2011, 36).

For Jacobs (2003, 7), the general failure of postsettlement support stems from a failure to conceptualize land reform beyond the land transfer stage, and from poor communication between the national DLA (responsible for land reform) and the nine provincial departments of agriculture (responsible for state services to farmers): "The rigid distinction in South Africa's land policy between land delivery and agricultural development has resulted in post-transfer support being largely neglected. There is no comprehensive policy on support for agricultural development after land transfer and the agencies entrusted with this function have made little progress in this regard. Agricultural assistance for individual land reform projects is ad hoc."

This lack of coordination between the key Departments of Agriculture and of Land Affairs is compounded by poor communication with other institutions (such as the Department of Housing and the Department of Water Affairs and Forestry) and local government structures (Hall, Isaacs, and Saruchera 2004). The need for additional support for land reform beneficiaries was acknowledged by the Ministry of Agriculture and Land Affairs, which led to the introduction in the fiscal 2004/05 national budget of both the Comprehensive Agricultural Support Program—a grant targeted to existing black farmers and the beneficiaries of land reform, largely intended for the development of infrastructure, with a total of R 750 million allocated over five years—and the Micro-Agricultural Finance Schemes of South Africa, intended to provide small loans to farmers (Hall and Lahiff 2004). The limited evidence available, however, would suggest that these measures are not reaching their intended targets or impacting significantly the generally low levels of production that persist across the majority of all land reform projects. In June 2011 the Minister of Agriculture announced that the Department of Agriculture planned to establish 50,000 commercial farmers within the former homelands and would make funding available under various headings to support small farmers: R 1 billion for CASP (Comprehensive Agricultural Support Programme), R 400 million for Ilima/Letsema (a Land and Agrarian Reform Program aimed at increasing food production), and R 57.7 million for the LandCare program of natural resource conservation.[16]

The well-developed (private) agribusiness sector that services large-scale commercial agriculture has shown no more than a token interest in extending its operations to new farmers who, in most cases, would be incapable of paying for such services anyway. The assumption that the private sector would somehow "respond" to demand from land reform beneficiaries with very different needs from the established commercial farmers has not been supported by recent experience. The principal explanation for that, of course, is that cash-strapped land reform beneficiaries generally are not in a position to exert any effective demand for the services on offer, even if those services are geared to their specific needs.

The widely reported problems faced by newly resettled farmers—which can be attributed to shortages of finance, possibly of skills, and certainly of appropriate support services—has led state agencies to adopt some innovative approaches, particularly in the context of the PLAS introduced in 2006. Under PLAS, beneficiaries are expected to prove their farming capacity during the initial period of leasehold, after which they can be granted ownership of the land at the discretion of state officials and dependent on their access to redistribution grants and other finance. Concerns have been raised, however, that denial of land title during the initial settlement phase and uncertainty about long-term ownership are making it even more difficult for resettled farmers to access finance, not least from the state-owned Land Bank. Moreover, the requirement that new farmers demonstrate profitability within a three- (or five-) year period is widely seen as unrealistic for an agricultural start-up. As a result, serious doubts persist that the conditions imposed under PLAS will actually deliver more sustainable and productive land use.

Up to about 2007, redistributed land was generally transferred directly to the grant-approved beneficiaries in freehold title. This was seen by some policy makers and others as problematic in cases where beneficiaries were unable or unwilling to make productive use of the land, whether because of shortages of capital or skills, tensions within beneficiary groups, or—most commonly—a lack of the promised support from government agencies. The introduction of PLAS—under which land title is held by the state—has effectively changed beneficiaries from landowners to tenants, allowing the state to impose more stringent requirements in terms of how land is used and, where desired, to dispossess beneficiaries and allocate the land to others. This so-called "use it or lose it" policy was announced by then Minister Xingwana in March 2009 and led to the high-profile eviction of a woman farmer in Gauteng Province, an action later challenged in the courts. The "use it or lose it" policy was subsequently reiterated by Minister Nkwinti, who advocated the rehabilitation of failing redistribution projects—which he estimated at 90 percent—through the program of Recapitalization and Development and the involvement of strategic partners.[17] This approach has particular implications for those receiving land leases under PLAS, and it remains to be seen how effective it might be in cases where occupiers hold freehold title.

## The Way Forward and Recent Institutional and Policy Development

This section addresses some of the key challenges that need to be addressed to deliver substantial areas of land to landless people in a sustainable manner and briefly reviews some recent institutional and policy developments.

### Agrarian Restructuring

As outlined above, the historical pace of redistributing land from white to black ownership has been exceedingly slow and appears to have slowed in recent years;[18] major concerns have been expressed at all levels about the quality of land involved and the prices paid for it.

Although many of these problems can be traced back to specific policy design weaknesses or poor implementation, the prolonged underperformance of the land reform program suggests a more fundamental dilemma—starting with the lack of a comprehensive vision of the kind of agrarian restructuring that is desired, of the means by which it is to be carried out, and of the intended beneficiaries. The Comprehensive Rural Development Program (CRDP)

Agricultural Land Redistribution and Land Administration in Sub-Saharan Africa
http://dx.doi.org/10.1596/978-1-4648-0188-4

launched by President Zuma in 2009 appears to address a wide range of issues across the agrarian economy, but the program is still at a pilot stage and currently focuses on the former homeland areas. Although reform here is an urgent priority, addressing the homelands in isolation from the much larger commercial farming areas—where land reform is taking place—can do little to further the overall restructuring of agrarian relations in South Africa. AgriBEE and other measures that address the advanced agribusiness sector have created opportunities for some new black entrepreneurs and shareholders, but have brought little direct benefit to the beneficiaries—or potential beneficiaries—of land reform.

Land expropriation—as provided for under the constitution—continues to be alluded to by a range of actors, including senior policy makers and the ANC Youth League, but does not appear to be a serious possibility at this point.[19] New policy initiatives such as PLAS continue to operate within the WSWB paradigm, to the distinct advantage of white landowners, and, to date, appear to have achieved little in terms of resolving the widely recognized problems at the heart of South Africa's land reform program. Various challenges to the existing pattern of landholding continue to circulate within political debates, including restricting landownership by foreigners, imposing a land tax, and nationalizing land, but none of these appears likely to be implemented in the near future.[20] Moreover, it is not clear how, if at all, such measures might contribute to a restructuring of landholding in favor of the poor and landless.

Overall, a comprehensive restructuring of landholding—such as envisaged under the 30 percent target—remains highly unlikely. Few if any measures exist that prioritize access to land for poor and marginalized groups: indeed, groups such as farm workers and labor tenants—who would appear to many to be ideal candidates for land reform—have seen a steady deterioration in their land rights since 1994.

### Institutional Reforms

The ANC and the government have increasingly recognized the importance and urgency of addressing rural development and land reform–related challenges. Since 2009 the government has adopted a two-pronged response to the challenges discussed in the previous sections. First, it has implemented institutional reforms, most notably by establishing the DRDLR, tasked with developing and coordinating the relevant policy, legislative, institutional, and programmatic activities of different government agencies active in the rural sector. Second, it has engaged in new strategy development, actively prioritizing rural development and land reform initiatives in all major economic development strategies, such as the Medium Term Strategic Framework (2010–14), Outcome 7 of the Delivery Agreement between the President and Ministers, the New Growth Plan, and the newly released National Development Plan (Vision 2030). However, as the past record clearly demonstrates, sustained commitment to, unwavering implementation of, and strong capacity to mobilize resources for the relevant strategies are the government's weakest points.

The new DRDLR is implementing a CRDP. Its strategic objective is to create vibrant and sustainable rural communities, achieved through a three-pronged strategy based on (1) a coordinated and integrated broad-based agrarian transformation, (2) accelerated rural development, and (3) an improved land reform program. Agrarian transformation will focus on the establishment of rural business initiatives, agro-industries, cooperatives, cultural initiatives, and vibrant local markets in rural settings; the empowerment of rural people and communities; and the revitalization of old and revamping of new economic and social infrastructures in rural areas. The efforts in rural development will enable rural people, through a participatory approach, to take control of their destiny, thereby dealing effectively with rural poverty through the optimal use and management of natural resources. Land reform efforts will focus on accelerating the pace of redistribution and land tenure reform and speeding up the settlement of outstanding land restitution claims by reviewing existing programs as well as associated legislation and policies.

Although it may be too early to reach a definite conclusion on the effectiveness of the institutional reforms, the reform does not seem to have generated many positive changes to date. Preliminary analysis suggests the following reasons for lack of the positive impact: First, the capacity of the DRDLR is relatively weak, and it will take time to strengthen it. As demonstrated internationally, successfully addressing rural development and land reform challenges requires a high capacity. It is argued that there are three major aspects for which capacity should be strengthened: (1) the DRDLR needs to develop an accurate, updated, and detailed understanding of the structure of South Africa's rural sector and the nature of its transformation, (2) there is an urgent need to develop a more focused and action-oriented mind-set, and (3) there is a need to establish a well-functioning M&E system.

Second, the DRDLR needs to find an effective operational model to enable it to play two different functions well in parallel. In terms of rural development, the DRDLR will mainly play a "horizontal coordinating" role, given the wide spectrum of rural development issues; in terms of land reform, the DRDLR will mainly play a "vertical implementation role." These require different operational models and management skills.

Third, the DRDLR's budget allocation does not match the needs of the rural development and land reform program. As indicated by senior DRDLR officials, the DRDLR requested a budget of R 18.3 billion over a three-year period, but the National Treasury allocated a budget of only R 6.3 billion over this period. The DRDLR then requested an additional amount of R 4.4 billion largely for restitution, but was given only R 0.29 million; the majority of that was used to establish the new DRDLR after it was assigned the mandate for rural development. In short, the DRDLR does not have adequate funds to achieve all of its objectives. On the other hand, given the current macroeconomic situation as well as the past unsatisfactory performance of the DRDLR's programs, it is reasonable for the National Treasury to ask the DRDLR to demonstrate convincing evidence of progress before approving the additional budget request.

Agricultural Land Redistribution and Land Administration in Sub-Saharan Africa
http://dx.doi.org/10.1596/978-1-4648-0188-4

### The "Green Paper on Land Reform"

The DRDLR released a draft "Green Paper on Land Reform" in early September 2011, and the public consultation process continued until January 2012. This section summarizes some comments from a review conducted by a group of international experts. The consensus is that the draft Green Paper could be significantly strengthened to serve as an adequate basis for improving South Africa's land reform programs.

Some experts (e.g., Chris Tanner) were encouraged to see that the Green Paper asserts that the land reform must be located within the CRDP. Land management and administration cannot be implemented in isolation from wider rural (and urban) development strategies, which, of course, include a range of other governance and socioeconomic investment elements.

Many experts (e.g., John Bruce and Hans Binswanger) were of the view that the Green Paper appears more interested in creating a land bureaucracy than achieving agrarian reform. More justifications are needed to support the proposed institutional changes. It is believed that the DRDLR could have benefited more from the very considerable amount of serious thinking done in South Africa in recent years about how to improve land policies. In addition, a clear exposition of issues should be added to the Green Paper (Hans Binswanger-Mkhize and Kay Leresche).

Many argued that the powers given to the Land Management Commission are worrisome, particularly the power of "verifying and/or validating/invalidating individual or corporate title deeds" and "seizing or confiscating land gotten through fraudulent or corrupt means" (e.g., John Bruce, Gavin Adlington, and Tony Lamb). These provisions could raise serious rule of law/constitutional issues. Similarly, the powers given to the Land Rights Management Board (LRMB) are also of concern, particularly the power to dissolve the Land Rights Management Committees (LRMCs) and overturn their decisions. It is clear that the LRMCs are not intended to function with any degree of autonomy, but are simply to be extensions of the LRMB. This appears to be inconsistent with the existing knowledge about what works well in local land institutions.

Most experts believed that the review of land reform experiences elsewhere could be improved considerably. For example, the description of China's recent reforms and Mexico's constitutional reform could be better presented. They also advised the DRDLR to look at experiences in Malawi, Mozambique, and Namibia, because these countries can provide examples more relevant to the Sub-Sahara Africa (SSA) context. In addition, discussions on the experiences from other countries should have specifically highlighted those aspects of direct relevance to the Green Paper's proposal.

Some experts (e.g., Hans Binswanger-Mkhize, Kay Leresche) pointed out that the Green Paper is basically silent on the following important topics: (1) the role and modalities of expropriation, as requested by the 2005 Land Summit; (2) the land tax (also requested by the Land Summit and on which the DRDLR has conducted an extensive consultation process, with support from the World Bank via including a major land tax paper); (3) the farming models to be pursued (collective, large-scale, or small and individual enterprise); (4) the all-important nonland components of land reform; (5) beneficiary identification and selection; (6) implementation options and modalities, such as stakeholder-driven land reform; and (7) implementation capacity and how to strengthen it. Successful land reform and agrarian transformation in South Africa will depend on effectively addressing these topics.

## Conclusions

Based on the above discussions, the major lessons offered by the implementation of South Africa's land reform program in the past 18 years can be summarized as the following:

- *Market-based reform alone does not work:* Market-based transactions present valuable opportunities for land redistribution in the South African context, whether between private sellers/buyers or via the state. However, the WSWB approach, applied since 1994, has clearly not worked as envisaged by its proponents. Although efforts have been made to rebrand the WSWB approach through programs such as PLAS, the fundamentals remain largely unchanged, pointing to the need for more radical change in key areas. Market purchases from "willing sellers" must be supported by genuinely proactive interventions by the state to acquire appropriate land for clearly identified beneficiaries at affordable prices. Selective expropriation and systematic subdivision of large farms would be central to this approach.

- *Need for appropriate legislation and rigorous application:* Section 25 of the South African constitution provides the basis for a potentially far-reaching land reform program, but is short on specifics. More details on the rights and obligations of various parties—including the state, property owners, and potential beneficiaries—and the methods to be used need to be set out in additional legislation, but this has largely not happened to date. The key lesson here is that the fundamentals of a program of land reform must be clearly set out in legislation—with amendments as circumstances change—and vigorously applied. Such legislation, and the political debates surrounding it, will help clarify the roles—and legitimate expectations—of state agencies and private citizens alike, and create the basis for a more integrated, and participatory, program of land reform.

- *Less of a focus on land acquisition and ownership, and more on land use:* Much attention has been given over the past 18 years to the formal aspects of property rights, whereas land use has been widely ignored or treated in a formulaic manner. An alternative approach would involve a more pragmatic approach to land acquisition, through significantly strengthening communities' participation. On the beneficiary side, this would involve building on existing farming practices and responding to clearly identified needs, provision of appropriately sized holding (based on subdivision of large farms), and greater flexibility around land use (e.g., accommodating both "commercial" and "subsistence" farming, and stages in between). Beneficiaries should have the option to acquire land on a lease-hold basis; where possible, group landholding or collective farming should be avoided.

- *Capacity strengthening to the bureaucracy:* A key lesson of South Africa's experience with land reform is that capacity of the state agencies involved—the national DRDLR (formally the DLA) and its branch the Commission on Restitution of Land Rights—and the provincial departments of agriculture has not been equal to the task. Three main areas of activity can be identified that require attention: land acquisition and transfer, farm planning and beneficiary approval, and postsettlement support. The existing range of state support services—based on the agricultural departments of the pre-1994 provinces and homelands—continue to perform extremely poorly and urgently need to be restructured and reoriented to offer effective support to small-scale and emerging farmers

- *Give a greater role to civil society:* Civil society organizations, and intended beneficiaries themselves, have been marginalized throughout the period of land reform. After the initial lodgement of land claims or applications for redistribution grants, the processes of land acquisition, farm planning, and project implementation have been dominated by state agencies—and their hired consultants—often with poor outcomes in terms of land utilization and livelihood improvements. More flexible, less formal, systems are required that would allow would-be beneficiaries and supportive organizations such as trade unions and rural NGOs a greater role in the selection of both land and beneficiaries, in the negotiation of land prices, and in project design. Mobilization of civil society in support of land reform would provide a more accurate indication of the level of demand for land (which may be quite limited) and increase the political pressure on landowners and state agencies to deliver more appropriate and sustainable land reform projects.

- *Postsettlement support is key to long-term success*: Postsettlement support is perhaps the weakest aspect of the South African land reform program to date. As indicated above, the institutional arrangements for the delivery of support services to resettled farmers are largely dysfunctional and the services provided have been neither adequate nor appropriate. Anecdotal evidence suggests that where new farmers are successfully established, it often depends on personal relationships between resettled farmers and local agricultural officials offering an old-fashioned extension service, involving frequent farm visits, establishment of relationships of trust, and advice that is appropriate to the level of skills and resources of the farmers concerned. This contrasts with the elaborate—and costly—"farm plans" imposed by state agencies on many resettled farmers, which typically collapse after a short time, leading to a breakdown of relationships and abandonment of the project by the agencies. Extension agents should work with farmers to develop affordable and sustainable land use. Production credit, which along with advice services is the most pressing need of most land reform beneficiaries, should be provided by a specialist agency under terms that are appropriate to small-scale and emerging farmers.

Land reform is an important aspect of social and economic transformation in South Africa, as a means of both redressing past injustices and alleviating the pressing problems of poverty and inequality in rural areas. The South African land reform program is founded on the country's constitution and has the potential for far-reaching change through restitution, tenure reform, and redistribution. The government's policies and associated implementation, however, have not generated expected results for numerous reasons and have fallen significantly short of their delivery targets. Even where land has been transferred, it appears to have had minimal impact on the livelihoods of beneficiaries, largely because of inappropriate project design, a lack of necessary support services, and shortages of working capital, leading to widespread underutilization of land. There is no evidence to suggest that land reform has led to improvements in agricultural efficiency, income, employment, or economic growth. Some gains undoubtedly have been made, but they remain largely at a symbolic level. Where real material advances have occurred, they often can be attributed to the involvement of third parties—individual mentors, agribusiness corporations, NGOs, or ecotourism investors.

The evidence of the last 18 years suggests that the current approach—based on acquisition of land through the open market, minimal support to new farmers, and bureaucratic imposition of production models loosely based on existing commercial operators—is unlikely to transform the rural economy and lift people out of poverty. What clearly is missing at present is any small-farmer path to development that could enable the millions of households residing in communal areas and on commercial farms to expand their own production and accumulate wealth and resources in an incremental manner. Without a doubt, making this happen would require radical restructuring of existing farm units to create family-size farms, more realistic farm planning, appropriate support from a much-reformed state agricultural service, and a much greater role for beneficiaries in the design and implementation of their own projects.

The effectiveness of recent institutional reforms and policy proposals—which focus mainly on the wider process of rural development, the process of land acquisition, and possible further institutional changes in land administration systems—remains to be seen. Another aspect clearly missing from the governance tradition is the sustained focus on implementation, resource mobilization, and timely policy adjustment. Much more will be required if South Africa's land-based economy is to contribute significantly to economic growth and to the redistribution of wealth and opportunities to the majority of the South African population.

Agricultural Land Redistribution and Land Administration in Sub-Saharan Africa
http://dx.doi.org/10.1596/978-1-4648-0188-4

## Notes

1. In 1996 the South African Census reported a total population of 40.5 million, broken down in the following terms: African for 76.7 percent; white, 10.9 percent; colored, 8.9 percent; Indian/Asian, 2.6 percent; and unspecified, 0.9 percent (Statistics South Africa 1996).

2. Agriculture accounted for 10 percent of formal employment in 2002 (Vink and Kirsten 2003, 6).

3. Constitution of the Republic of South Africa. 1996. http://www.info.gov.za/documents /constitution/.

4. Of these, 4,680 were settled through restoration of land, 4,695 by financial compensation (i.e., no land), and 436 by alternative remedies (mostly housing in public projects).

5. Of the estimated 2,351,086 people displaced from farms since 1994, a total of 942,303 (40 percent) were found to have been evicted; others left for a variety of other social and economic reasons (Wegerif, Russell, and Grundling 2005, 7).

6. Cousins and Hall (2011, 14) point to widespread failure of the policy, a decade of fruitless policy review, ongoing evictions of farm dwellers, and a general shift away from the language of rights to one of productivity and economic efficiency.

7. Stephan Hofstatter, "South Africa: Back to Land-Policy Drawing Board," *Business Day*, February 18, 2010.

8. Report by the Director General of DLA to the Parliamentary Portfolio Committee on Agriculture and Land Affairs, "Didiza Offers Reasons for Limpopo Failures," quoted in *Farmers Weekly*, November 18, 2005.

9. Speech by Rural Development and Land Reform Minister, Gugile Nkwinti, on his departmental budget vote, National Assembly, Parliament, Cape Town, June 17, 2009.

10. In 2010/11, for example, only 3,089 beneficiaries were reported under PLAS, in 288 projects (DRDLR 2011).

11. Unlike the situation in such countries as Brazil, India, and Malawi, the self-selection process in South Africa lacks a strong element of oversight by communities, labor unions, and other civil society organizations, reflecting the generally low level of popular participation in the implementation of land reform in the country.

12. For example, labor tenants (that is, tenant farmers) in Mpumalanga, with a long history of family-based farming, have been resettled in groups on specially acquired farms, which they hold collectively in undivided shares—effectively, a forced collectivization.

13. This discussion focuses on the failure to subdivide farms after they have been acquired. However, a policy of acquiring portions of farms, in sizes appropriate to the needs of identified beneficiaries, could make the acquisition process itself much quicker and the land reform program more attractive to more people. Thus, the failure to subdivide contributes not only to postacquisition failures of production, but also to the slow pace of land transfer.

14. International experiences, particularly those from the former Soviet Union and China, clearly demonstrated that "forced collective production" causes serious efficiency loss and is not sustainable. China's successful economic development in the past three decades started with dismantling people's communes (which organized collective production at the village level) and introducing household-based production systems.

15. Report by the Director General of DLA to the Parliamentary Portfolio Committee on Agriculture and Land Affairs, "Didiza Offers Reasons for Limpopo Failures," quoted in *Farmers Weekly*, November 18, 2005.

16. "Government to Establish 50,000 Smallholder Farmers," BuaNews online, www .buanews.gov.za/news/11/11061515451001.

17. Government Communication and Information System online, March 5, 2009, "Government to Confiscate Farms Left Undeveloped by Beneficiaries," http://www .buanews.gov.za/news/09/09030510451003; "Minister Takes Land Back from New Black Owner," *Business Day*, April 9, 2009; "90% of Redistributed Farms Not Functional—Nkwinti," *Sapa*, March 3, 2010. http://www.politicsweb.co.za/politicsweb /view/politicsweb/en/page72308?oid=163515&sn=Marketingweb_detail.

18. In 2007/08, only 432,226 hectares were redistributed under "Land Reform" compared to an official target of 2.5 million ha (DLA 2008); the following year, a similar figure of 443,600 hectares were redistributed versus the target for the year of 1,500,000 hectares (DRDLR 2009, 33); in 2009/10, 239,990 ha were transferred/acquired out of a target of 656,000 (DRDLR 2010, 28); in 2010/11, the target was greatly reduced to 283,592 hectares, which on this occasion was exceeded by 14 percent (DRDLR 2011, 35).

19. For example, in July 2011, the Minister for Rural Development and Land Reform was quoted in the press as saying that expropriation of land without compensation is a possibility in future ("Land Must Be Given Back Fast," *City Press*, July 10, 2011), http://www.citypress.co.za/Politics/News/Land-must-be-given-back-fast-20110709.

20. In January 2011 President Zuma told the ANC that he was once again considering a ban on foreign ownership of land. See AFP, "S. Africa May Restrict Foreign Land Ownership," January 8, 2011, http://www.google.com/hostednews/afp/article /ALeqM5gm8n-OpWzZOhl-0qHsEHukwSTaLw?docId=CNG.a27b39ffaaaac7cc 869cca243268ca85.581.

## References

Ahmed, A., P. Jacobs, R. Hall, W. Kapery, R. Omar, and M. Schwartz. 2003. *Monitoring and Evaluating the Quality of Life of Land Reform Beneficiaries: 2000/2001*. Technical report prepared for the Department of Land Affairs, Directorate of Monitoring and Evaluation, Pretoria.

ANC (African National Congress). 1994. *The Reconstruction and Development Programme: A Policy Framework*. Johannesburg, South Africa: Umanyano.

Bradstock, A. 2005. *Key Experiences of Land Reform in the Northern Cape Province of South Africa*. London: FARM-Africa.

Claassens, A., and B. Cousins, eds. 2008. *Land, Power and Custom: Controversies Generated by South Africa's Communal Land Rights Act*. Cape Town: UCT Press; Athens, OH: Ohio University Press.

Cousins, B. 2007. "More Than Socially Embedded: The Distinctive Character of 'Communal Tenure' Regimes in South Africa and Its Implications for Land Policy." *Journal of Agrarian Change* 7 (3): 281–315.

Cousins, B., and R. Hall. 2011. "Rights without Illusions: The Potential and Limits of Rights-Based Approaches to Securing Land Tenure in Rural South Africa." Working Paper 18, PLAAS, University of the Western Cape, Cape Town.

Derman, B., E. Lahiff, and E. Sjaastad. 2006. "Strategic Questions about Strategic Partners: Challenges and Pitfalls in South Africa's New Model of Land Restitution." Paper presented to the Land, Memory, Reconstruction and Justice Conference, Cape Town, September 13–15.

DRDLR (Government of South Africa, Department of Rural Development and Land Reform). 2009. *Annual Report 2008/09*. Pretoria.

———. 2010. *Annual Report 2009/2010*. Pretoria.

———. 2011. *Annual Report 2010/11*. Pretoria.

Government of South Africa, Department of Land Affairs. 1997. *White Paper on South African Land Policy*. Pretoria: Department of Land Affairs, Government of South Africa.

———. 2004. *The A-Z of the Communal Land Rights Act, 2004 (Act No. 11 of 2004)*. Pretoria. http://land.pwv.gov.za/tenurereform/.

———. 2005. "Delivery of Land and Agrarian Reform." Report to the National Land Summit, Johannesburg, South Africa, July 27–31.

———. 2008. *Annual Report April 2007–March 2008*. Pretoria.

Hall, R. 2003. *Farm Tenure*. Evaluating Land and Agrarian Reform in South Africa Series, Report 3, Programme for Land and Agrarian Studies, University of the Western Cape, Cape Town, South Africa.

———. 2004a. *Land and Agrarian Reform in South Africa: A Status Report 2004*. Research Report 20, Programme for Land and Agrarian Studies, University of the Western Cape, Cape Town, South Africa.

———. 2004b. *LRAD Rapid Systematic Assessment Survey: Nine Case Studies in the Eastern Cape*. Unpublished manuscript, Programme for Land and Agrarian Studies, University of the Western Cape, Cape Town, South Africa.

Hall, R., M. Isaacs, and M. Saruchera. 2004. *Land and Agrarian Reform in Integrated Development Plans: Case Studies from Selected District and Local Municipalities*. Unpublished manuscript, Programme for Land and Agrarian Studies, University of the Western Cape, Cape Town, South Africa.

Hall, R., P. Jacobs, and E. Lahiff. 2003. *Final Report*. Evaluating Land and Agrarian Reform in South Africa Series, Report 10, Programme for Land and Agrarian Studies, University of the Western Cape, Cape Town, South Africa.

Hall, R., and E. Lahiff. 2004. "Budgeting for Land Reform." Policy Brief 13, Programme for Land and Agrarian Studies, University of the Western Cape, Cape Town, South Africa.

HSRC (Human Sciences Research Council). 2003. *Land Redistribution for Agricultural Development: Case Studies in Three Provinces*. Unpublished manuscript. Integrated Rural and Regional Development Division, Pretoria.

Human Rights Watch. 2011. *Ripe with Abuse: Human Rights Conditions in South Africa's Fruit and Wine Industries*. New York: Human Rights Watch. http://www.hrw.org/sites /default/files/reports/safarm0811webwcover.pdf.

Jacobs, P. 2003. *Support for Agricultural Development*. Evaluating Land and Agrarian Reform in South Africa Series, Report 4, Programme for Land and Agrarian Studies, University of the Western Cape, Cape Town, South Africa.

Kleinbooi, K., E. Lahiff, and T. Boyce. 2006. *Land Reform, Farm Employment and Livelihoods. Western Cape Case Study: Theewaterskloof Local Municipality*. Programme for Land and Agrarian Studies, University of the Western Cape, Cape Town, and Human Sciences Research Council, Pretoria.

Lahiff, E. 2007. "State, Market or the Worst of Both? Experimenting with Market-Based Land Reform in South Africa." Occasional Paper 30, Programme for Land and Agrarian Studies, University of the Western Cape, Cape Town, South Africa.

Lahiff, E., N. Davis, and T. Manenzhe. 2012. *Joint Ventures in Agriculture: Lessons from Land Reform Projects in South Africa*. London: IIED/IFAD/FAO/PLAAS.

Lyne, M. C., and M. A. G. Darroch. 2003. "Land Redistribution in South Africa: Past Performance and Future Policy." BASIS CRSP Research Paper, Department of Agricultural and Applied Economics, University of Wisconsin–Madison.

May, J., and B. Roberts. 2000. *Monitoring and Evaluating the Quality of Life of Land Reform Beneficiaries: 1998/1999*. Summary Report prepared for the Department of Land Affairs. Pretoria: Department of Land Affairs.

Mayson, D. 2003. *Joint Ventures*. Evaluating Land and Agrarian Reform in South Africa Series, Report 7, Programme for Land and Agrarian Studies, University of the Western Cape, Cape Town, South Africa.

NDA (National Department of Agriculture). 2005. *Abstract of Agricultural Statistics*. Pretoria: Directorate, Agricultural Statistics, National Department of Agriculture.

Ntsebeza, L. 2006. *Democracy Compromised: Chiefs and the Politics of the Land in South Africa*. Cape Town, South Africa: HSRC Press.

———. 2007. "Land Redistribution in South Africa: The Property Clause Revisited." In *The Land Question in South Africa: The Challenge of Transformation and Redistribution*, edited by L. Ntsebeza and R. Hall, 107–131. Cape Town, South Africa: HSRC Press.

OECD (Organisation for Economic Co-operation and Development). 2006. *OECD Review of Agricultural Policies: South Africa*. Paris: OECD.

Statistics South Africa. 1996. The People of South Africa Population Census. Pretoria.

———. 2006. *Annual Report 2005/2006*. Pretoria.

Tilley, S. 2004. *Why Do the Landless Remain Landless? An Examination of Land Acquisition and the Extent to Which the Land Market and Land Redistribution Mechanisms Serve the Needs of Land-Seeking People*. Research Report, Surplus People Project, Cape Town, South Africa.

van den Brink, R., G. S. Thomas, and H. Binswanger. 2007. "Agricultural Land Redistribution in South Africa: Towards Accelerated Implementation." In *The Land Question in South Africa: The Challenge of Transformation and Redistribution*, edited by L. Ntsebeza and R. Hall, 152–201. Cape Town, South Africa: HSRC Press.

Vink, N., and J. Kirsten. 2003. "Agriculture in the National Economy." In *The Challenge of Change: Agriculture, Land and the South African Economy*, edited by L. Nieuwoudt and J. Groenewald, 3–20. Scottsville, South Africa: University of Natal Press.

Walker, C. 2003. "Piety in the Sky? Gender Policy and Land Reform in South Africa." *Journal of Agrarian Change* 3 (1–2): 111–48.

Wegerif, M. 2004. *A Critical Appraisal of South Africa's Market-Based Land Reform Policy: The Case of the Land Redistribution for Agricultural Development (LRAD) Program in Limpopo*. Research Report 19, Programme for Land and Agrarian Studies, University of the Western Cape, Cape Town.

Wegerif, M., B. Russell, and I. Grundling. 2005. *Summary of Key Findings from the National Evictions Survey*. Polokwane, South Africa: Nkuzi Development Association.

Williams, G. 1996. "Setting the Agenda: A Critique of the World Bank's Rural Restructuring Programme for South Africa." *Journal of Southern African Studies* 22 (1): 139–67.

World Bank. 1994. "South African Agriculture: Structure, Performance and Options for the Future." Working Paper 12950, World Bank, Washington, DC.

———. 2008. *World Development Report: Agriculture for Development*. Washington, DC: World Bank.

Xaba, Z. 2004. "Living in the Shadow of Democracy." *AFRA News* 57 (May). http://www .afra.co.za/default.asp?id=1015.

# CHAPTER 3

# Decentralization of Land Administration in Sub-Saharan Africa: Recent Experiences and Lessons Learned

John Bruce

## Introduction

Land administration is a key land governance function, a role played by the state in many countries by documenting and protecting rights in land and by facilitating the operation of markets in land rights. There is broad recognition that the documentation and formalization of land rights in Africa is a key development challenge, but less agreement as to how to go about it effectively. Decentralization of land administration is an important element in the discussion of how best to move forward. Ribot (2001, 2) makes a succinct case for decentralization: "The underlying developmentalist logic of decentralization is that local institutions can better discern and are more likely to respond to local needs and aspirations. Theorists believe this ability derives from local authorities having better access to information and being more easily held accountable to local populations." Land is ineffably local, sited in local communities, and this gives a special logic to decentralization of land administration.

But decentralization does not come easily. Central government agencies asked to let go of prerogatives and funding may resist. Moreover, in most of Africa, land administration is already effectively decentralized to traditional authorities administering land under custom, with or without legal foundation in national law. The fact that those traditional authorities have full information about local landholding, while the state lacks such information, has constrained the extension of state authority in this area and accounts for the failure of many centrally driven land programs. All of the decentralization programs reviewed in this case study are being conducted in the programmatic context of survey and registration of landholdings, which would provide the state with the land information it now largely lacks. When land administration decentralization strategies seek to undermine traditional authorities, whose power is based largely on control of land, the change is part of a larger struggle for authority and is politically charged.

Efforts to decentralize authority over land in Africa tend to adopt one of four basic strategies (Bruce and Knox 2009): (1) replicating locally, with some simplification, existing offices of the central government's land agency and granting them limited administrative autonomy; (2) creating more modest and more locally representative specialized bodies at the community level, such as community land boards or committees; (3) decentralizing authority over land to nonspecialized local civil authorities, such as local councils, possibly with the creation of a subcommittee or other subsidiary unit for handling land matters; and/or (4) relying upon traditional authorities as the lowest rung of land administration. Some countries adopt a combination of these approaches, but usually one basic thrust is discernible.

For the purposes of this case study, the experiences of four countries with quite different decentralization programs are reviewed:

- In Uganda, the Land Act of 1998 envisaged an ambitious decentralization involving both expansion of registration and related services for formalization of customary rights and the creation of local land committees and a hierarchy of other institutions, including specialized land dispute settlement institutions.
- In Tanzania, the Village Land Act of 1999 provided for a major vesting of land administration tasks in villages, as well as expansion of land services, with stress on implementation upon demarcation and registration of village and household lands.
- In Ethiopia, under both national legislation and state laws in this federal system, important land administration functions are vested at the local level, including key roles in the implementation of an ambitious program of mapping and certifying household landholdings.
- In Ghana, customary land tenure is legally recognized and governs over 80 percent of rural land, and the government is creating customary land secretariats (CLSs) to build capacity, transparency, and accountability in customary land administration; at the same time, it is piloting systematic registration of customary and statutory land rights.

Although these examples do not exhaust the diversity of approaches taken, they do provide an adequate basis on which to develop a discussion of most pros and cons of various approaches to decentralization.[1] Thus, this case study seeks to assess the effectiveness of the different approaches, examining in each of the four countries the following:

- The land administration roles decentralized and by whom they will be performed.
- The interactions between (1) the decentralized land administration institutions and those at higher levels and (2) the decentralized land administration

institutions and other local institutions, in particular those with land management roles.

- The extent to which the decentralization is a deconcentration or a devolution of authority.
- The sustainability in management and financial terms of each system as decentralized.

It is worth stressing at the outset that there is no one "best" practice with regard to decentralization of land administration. There are perfectly reasonable bases for selecting different approaches for different national contexts, reflecting fiscal, legal, political, and cultural considerations. The primary concern of this study is to understand the relative costs, benefits, pitfalls, and opportunities involved in the different approaches.

## Uganda's Experience with Decentralization

Uganda's 1995 constitution and 1998 Land Act vest land in the citizens of Uganda, recognizing public, private, and customary ownership of land. The introduction of title registration on the Torrens model at the end of the Buganda War under the 1900 Buganda Agreement and its systematic application in the Buganda Kingdom gave Uganda a local form of freehold called *mailo*. *Mailo* and other freehold tenure together cover about 18 percent of the country, with about 700,000 titles. Land in urban areas, some government-owned land, and land held by noncitizens are held under 99-year leaseholds. Customary rights apply to about 62 percent of the land and about 68 percent of the population, which accounts for approximately 8 million customary landholders throughout Uganda. Those rights were until recently not registrable interests and could be registered only in conversion to freehold. Registration of a certificate of customary ownership is now allowed by law, but few of these have been issued or registered (Burns 2007). Uganda's land administration system needs to accommodate the recording of a mass of transfers of land rights, principally alienations and leases of public land, sales, leases, and mortgages of freehold and *mailo* lands, reallocations of customary rights, and the inheritance of land under all categories of ownership.

In part because of the extended conflict in Uganda in the 1980s, Uganda has had to rebuild its land administration system. The Ministry of Lands, Housing and Urban Development is responsible for land management, registration, mapping, surveying, and valuation of properties, coordination, and supervision. The rebuilding of the system is still a work in progress. Only 5–6 percent of the titleholders have current titles, mostly concentrated in urban areas and in Buganda (Bruce and Mighot-Adholla 1994; Burns 2007).

Decentralization has been declared government policy since the Museveni government assumed power in 1986, creating a system of local councils initially closely tied to the Uganda National Resistance Movement. Later, in local government laws enacted in 1993 and 1997, these councils were made part of the regular system of local government. Impressive progress has been made in both administrative and fiscal decentralization, with local government employees now constituting 75 percent of the public service and 38 percent of the national budget now allocated to local government (Okidi and Guloba 2006).

The Land Act of 1998 provided for an ambitious decentralization of the land sector. The act outlined the extensive staffing requirements of the decentralized system, in both registry offices and local land boards and committees. The full-time staffing requirements nationwide totaled 20,000 positions (McAuslan 2003). When costs were calculated—after enactment of the Land Act—operating costs alone were estimated at U Sh 19 billion per year (US$15.5 million), a figure that exceeded the annual budget for the responsible ministry.

The Land Sector Strategic Plan (LSSP) 2001–11 confirms Uganda's commitment to decentralization of land administration and proposes a streamlining of the administrative actors envisaged in the Land Act (Government of Uganda 2001). The Land (Amendment) Act of 2001 eliminated some staffing categories, giving flexibility in defining acceptable staff requirements of land registries; provided more discretion to districts regarding the level of subsidiary land administration units to be created; and relied more on existing administrative institutions with participation compensated by sitting allowances rather than salaries. The basic characteristics of the new system are the following:

- At the district level, District Land Boards are appointed by the District Council on the recommendation of the district executive committee, with the approval of the minister responsible for lands. The board holds and allocates public land, as well as facilitates land registration activities. A District Land Office staffed by the ministry provides technical services to the District Land Board.
- Each subcounty, town council/township, or division of a city has a land committee that consists of a chairperson and three other members, at least one of whom must be a woman. The land committees are appointed by the District Council and play an advisory and assistance role for the District Land Board.
- Land tribunals may be created at both the district and subcounty level, with appeals to the High Court.

Implementation began slowly. As of mid-2003, 45 District Land Boards and 56 district land tribunals had been established and funding released to support these bodies. The LSSP was prepared to provide necessary guidance for project implementation and financing. Funding projected for 2000–01 was U Sh 3 billion, rising to U Sh 10 billion over a 10-year period (US$1 = U Sh 2,523).[2] Some commentators have suggested that the gap of several years between the LSSP's issuance and implementation was costly in terms of loss of momentum and credibility of the new system (McAuslan 2003; Hunt 2004).

Substantial external funding for the decentralized land administration system, focused on various land sector problems but with a strong emphasis on title registration, became available in 2005 under the Land Component of the World Bank's Private Sector Competitiveness Project II (PSCP II). The project aimed to rehabilitate land registry offices, update land records, establish a modern land information system (LIS), and strengthen the capacity of the land registries to process and maintain land titles. It also aimed to upgrade land offices in districts with a large volume of land transactions, reestablish the survey school, sensitize the population on land tenure security, and extend formal land registration with titles and certificates of land occupancy and customary ownership throughout the country but with greater intensity in only eight districts. This included the full-scale reestablishment of primary and secondary geodetic control networks to ensure survey accuracy, conversion from manual records and operating procedures to electronic documents management and a computerized workflow management system, a training and land sector staff capacity building program, and a massive land literacy campaign.

By 2008 the project had completed the design and initiated the construction of eight new custom-built land offices and four renovations. Initial piloting of systematic land titling was carried out in Ntungamo, Masaka, Iganga, and Mbale. Preparations for scaling up operations in at least six districts simultaneously were under way. More than 7,300 transactions were recorded between July 2006 and January 2007. Under PSCP II the transactions completed from February to December 2007 jumped to more than 28,000. The reorganized access to land records and data entry had reduced the cost of doing business. The conversion from manual operations to an electronic records management system had progressed as scheduled, and 100 percent of Kampala and Wakiso's records were computerized. Full-scale computerization was completed in early 2013 in six zonal land offices (holding about three-quarters of the country's land records) as part of the LIS, which was initiated in March 2009 and completed in February 2013 (World Bank 2008a, 2008b).

However, difficulty had been seen in recruiting staff because of the scarcity of people with the required skills and competition with the private sector for them. This problem most acutely affected the District Land Offices, which in many cases lacked even the minimum complement of land officers. A funding shortfall also set back efforts for refurbishing and equipping land offices; plans had aimed at 21 offices, but the project budget was adequate for only 13. The goal of systematically demarcating and titling one parish in each of at least 14 districts was not met in many of them because this activity was underfunded. The acceptable cost range per parcel surveyed and registered had been established from pilot data at US$24–32, requiring a budget of US$3.584 million, but the project allocated only US$694,000 for the entire operation (World Bank 2008a, 2008b). A new private sector development project, which was approved in May 2013, contains a US$55 million land administration component to finance, among other things, systematic land titling, construction of new buildings for or rehabilitation of all 21 land offices in the districts' capitals (as they existed in 1971) to operate as zonal offices serving other districts within their range, and expansion of the LIS to cover those District Land Offices (World Bank 2013). Extending systematic land titling beyond the pilot districts to cover 14 new districts was also held back because, despite heavy investments in sensitization and awareness campaigns, the mistrust of government by local people who thought that it could grab their land was not overcome in all districts. To enhance success in raising aware-ness and sensitization about the goals of land titling and improved land adminis-tration services, implementation of field activities of the new project will be preceded by a Communication Strategy and a Civil Society Outreach Strategy (World Bank 2013).

The 2011 Uganda National Land Policy (UNLP) indicates a clear realization that the land administration system needs further work. To reform delivery of land services, the UNLP (paras. 100–103, 111) sets out the following changes in the ongoing program of decentralization:

- Review the Local Governments Act to delegate some of the land administra-tion and management functions to local governments;
- Create through an act of Parliament a semiautonomous "State Land Agency" responsible for land administration and management at the national level;
- Establish regional land offices appropriately located to deliver land services until such a time when each district can have a full-fledged District Land Office;
- Privatize a limited number of land rights delivery services under guidelines established by the semiautonomous State Land Agency; and
- Retain dispute processing functions in communities and decentralized state institutions established under the Land Act, reinstating the land tribunals, properly resourced,[3] and establishing a special division in the High Court and Magistrates Court to handle land disputes.

Revenue generation to support the system is also dealt with by the UNLP, though briefly. It notes that decentralization of land administration has created opportunities for revenue generation and fiscal management through land taxes, land rates, stamp duties, rental income, and charges for delivery of land services. It urges that the full potential to generate revenue be realized and proposes a number of measures to that end (paras. 114–115).

Uganda's decentralization efforts have had to struggle uphill against both budgetary constraints and limited numbers of staff with the needed technical capacity. This has been rendered more acute by a rapid expansion in the num-ber of districts. There were fewer than 60 in 1998 when the Land Act was passed, but 111 districts existed as of August 2010, and another 20 were expected in 2011. Although international donors can help establish new sys-tems, they cannot usually fund salaries, and projects provide only limited and time-bound support for operations. Privatizing some activities is a partial solu-tion, but the needed skills are often scarce in both the public and private sectors. For instance, there are only 50 registered land surveyors in Uganda (Byamugisha 2013). Efforts continue to enhance the technical skills and sys-tems for records of land rights that are basic to the land administration system. The World Bank funded a pilot phase to test a parcel-based LIS in six districts (six zonal offices) over three years, and this will be scaled up for implemen-tation nationally in 21 zonal land offices under the new project that was approved in May 2013 (World Bank 2013).

## *Assessment of Decentralization of Land Administration in Uganda*

This centrally planned and implemented extension of land registry services into rural Uganda and provincial cities has been closely tied to a program of systematic adjudication and registration of land rights. Its principal rationale is provision of services to those receiving registered titles, and marketability of those land rights will create a growing need for such services. District registries existed in Uganda even in the late colonial period, servicing *mailo* and freehold land, so the current decentralization can be seen in the context of a postconflict reconstruction.

Uganda's decentralization is taking place within a well-developed scheme for funding of district government activities. The role of district governments in funding the maintenance of the land administration system will give those governments an influence over its future operations, which will be counterbalanced by the central government's ability to influence this through provision of targeted subsidies to districts. Because customary rights are registrable under the Land Act, the potential exists for mutually reinforcing interactions with the community-level institutions created by that act to manage land under custom. The decentralization effort has not, however, sought to develop the capacity of those community institutions. The local availability of land administration services may in the end facilitate the work of those community institutions, but the interactions anticipated are not clearly spelled out in the program documents. Clarification is needed, particularly in light of the general intention expressed in the UNLP to use traditional authorities as the base for the land administration system. Uganda's decentralization of land administration is thus essentially a deconcentration of existing land administration roles to district offices, with little effort to use that process to realize the earlier devolution of land management roles to local statutory and customary authorities with regard to land under custom.

Sustainability has been a major issue for Uganda's title registration system in the past. The operational framework for shared funding by national and local governments makes the picture regarding financial sustainability hopeful. Districts' willingness to contribute to the expansion of the local registries will be an indicator of the priority they give to the system. The prospects for financial sustainability will improve if, as proposed in the UNLP, the government enacts a law establishing a semiautonomous state agency responsible for land administration and management at the national level, one that can retain fees and has considerable financial autonomy.

It is less clear that social sustainability is well catered for. There appears to be a significant popular demand for government documentation of land rights, and the program has devoted considerable resources to public education and sensitization. Sustainability will depend on whether these efforts have sparked development of a "culture of registration" in which landholders step up to register transfers and successions. The failure to build capacity in local land management institutions, statutory and customary, and the fuzziness of the stated relationship between local land management and land administration institutions require clarification. The decentralized registry system needs to be able to regularly access information on local landholdings and land rights held by other local institutions.

## Tanzania's Experience with Decentralization

Even during the colonial period, private ownership of land in Tanzania was severely limited, and it was abolished entirely shortly after independence by legislation converting private ownership into long-term, transferable use rights or, in some cases, leaseholds. The vast majority of land users who had held land under custom continued to have "deemed use rights" ("deemed" as opposed to documented). This recognition was based on possession rather than any general recognition of custom, but national law continued to allow custom to control successions to such land.

In the immediate postindependence period, the government's pursuit of socialism included a program to move households living scattered on farms into villages to promote service provision. This "villagization" led to painful relocations and a considerable degree of confusion over land rights; the controversy over land rights threatened to undo the entire program. A policy review was initiated in 1991 with the creation of a Presidential Commission of Inquiry on Land Matters (the "Shivji Commission"). The commission's report was groundbreaking in addressing land issues facing Tanzania (and other countries in the region as well) (Government of Tanzania 1994). It frankly documented the developments during and after the villagization program and grappled thoughtfully with the issues around customary rights in rural land. The government responded to the commission's recommendations with a 1995 National Land Policy and two critical enactments on land in 1999, the Village Land Act and the Land Act, the latter governing land in cities and other areas.

Under these acts, all land in Tanzania continues to be the property of the state, but with clear long-term use rights for private landholders. The categories of land tenure recognized in Tanzania today include transferable and inheritable use rights on both urban and village land, village land rights held by village councils, and public lands (divided into reserved lands: parks and reserves) and general land (unassigned public land held by the Commissioner of Lands). The current breakdown is: village land, 70 percent; reserved lands, 28 percent; and general lands, 2 percent (Government of Tanzania 2006).

When implementation of these new laws began, most property rights in land were not documented or mapped. Only about 150,000 land parcels were registered, and 90 percent of Tanzanians did not have their holdings shown on a property registry system. Various different record systems maintained information on rights in land. The Title Registry registered only leasehold rights and dealings in those rights, which were readily transferable and inheritable. The Survey and Mapping Division maintained information regarding survey plans. Today the Title Registry operates a central office in Dar es Salaam and five zonal offices. There are about 70,000 registered titles in Dar es Salaam and perhaps

100,000 nationally. Few of these titles are charted on index maps. The government recognizes that registration offices are understaffed and cramped (Government of Tanzania 2006).

Under the Village Land Act, the state retains residual title to village land, but customary rights in more than 11,000 villages are given legal recognition as statutory rights capable of certification and registration by the state. Village land administration is provided for in elaborate detail, and control over village lands is devolved to elected village land councils, which make allocation and other decisions regarding village lands and must report their dispositions to the village assembly. Village land councils have the power to regulate community land use through by-laws, but can exercise this authority only after village land has been surveyed and a Certificate of Village Land (CVL) issued, signed by the Commissioner of Lands. Certificates of Customary Rights of Occupancy (CCRO) for individual owners within a village are signed by the village president and countersigned by the district land registrar. Village-level land registries to record these are mandated, with duplicate registrations at the district level. Separate village land councils have mediation powers. The cost of implementation of the legal reforms was estimated at T Sh 2.8 billion (US$3.16 million) per year for the first four years (McAuslan 2003; Wily 2003b).

The extent to which these laws represent a substantial devolution and empowerment of communities has been much debated. The debate is summarized by Palmer (1999): Professor Issa Shivji, who chaired the Presidential Commission of Inquiry on Land Matters, has been disappointed by the failure of the subsequent land policy and land laws to vest full ownership of land in the village communities, and complains of "the enormous powers over the ownership, control and management of village lands placed in the hands of the Ministry, and through the Ministry, the Commissioner [of Lands]." He suggests that the village land council manages village land "more as an agent of the Commissioner rather than as an organ of the village accountable to the village community." Dr. Liz Wily, a long-term observer and knowledgeable commentator on Tanzanian land policy, is more optimistic. She argues that "The whole point of The Village Land Act is for devolved land administration, by the village, at the village, for the village." The distinctive nature of the Tanzanian law, she urges, is its "vesting of [most] control over land tenure administration at the grassroots in the hands of the 'governments' [village councils] elected by the members of each registered village community." The powers of the Commissioner are in fact ample, but come into play in limited circumstances, in particular when the central government takes advantage of the state's residual title to acquire community land for development projects.

Implementation of the Village Land Act proceeded slowly initially. The land administration provisions of the act require first surveying village land boundaries and issuing the village a CVL. Pilot projects were launched in Mbozi District in the Mbeya region. A few villages were adjudicated in 2002 and 2003, but it was not until March 2004 that the first CCROs were issued. During the first four years of implementation (to 2005), certification of village boundaries had been issued in only one district covering 36 villages, precluding nearly all villages from issuing CCROs to villagers. In these first four years, an average of T Sh 193.4 million per year was spent, far short of the estimated T Sh 2.8 billion needed per year (Msangi 2005). A 2005 assessment estimated that 167 villages (1.6 percent) had obtained an official CVL from the Minister of Lands (Instituto Liberdad y Democracia 2005, 26). European Union and Norwegian support of €1 million was provided for implementation in other districts and 15 districts were ultimately covered, but only a few CVLs had been issued when the funding was exhausted in 2008 (Pedersen 2010).

As a sense of the costs involved grew, the government realized that the lack of finances and actual administrative capacity necessary to implement the Village Land Act were going to be a major obstacle. At a 2005 symposium on implementation, the Permanent Secretary of the Ministry of Lands worried that "the cost of full implementation nationwide is staggering" and explained that difficulties in implementation stemmed from shortages of resources, especially the lack of village level maps. Participants expressed concern at the lack of capacity at the district level to implement the acts, the lack of central support for implementation-related tasks, and the lack of funding for adjudicative processes and tribunals (Knight 2010).

In response, five years after enactment of the laws by Parliament, the ministry produced a Strategic Plan in Implementation of Land Law (SPILL) in 2005. SPILL indicates how implementation activities should be prioritized, covering the period 2005/06–2014/15, and includes an investment plan. The main thrusts of SPILL are promoting efforts to curb explosive land conflicts, instituting limits on household landholding to ensure that more families can access land, increasing the number of registered villages, creating and delivering CCROs throughout Tanzania, setting up village land committees, and creating formal links between NGOs, community-based organizations, and District Land Offices to facilitate implementation (Knight 2010, 198). The investment plan incorporated in SPILL indicates that implementation will cost more than T Sh 300 billion, of which only about T Sh 3 billion are foreseen to come from the ordinary government budget. The remaining T Sh 297 billion will have to come from foreign assistance.

In 2004, influenced by the ideas of Peruvian economist Hernando de Soto, the President's Office initiated a Property and Business Formalization Program, known by its Swahili acronym MKURABITA. MKURABITA was funded by Norway and implemented by de Soto's Institute of Liberty and Democracy, with its institutional home in the President's Office, autonomous of the Ministry of Lands, Housing and Urban Development. It carried out numerous projects using the Land Acts as the framework for formalization; most notable were pilot projects in Handeni at the end of 2006 and in Bagamoyo in 2007–08 (Kosyando 2007, 2008). An assessment in 2008 (NORAD et al. 2008) led the Norwegian government to withdraw from the project. The funding of MKURABITA and the scope of its activities today is unclear (Pedersen 2010). Knight (2010, 202) remarks that although simplifying reforms are indeed needed, there appears be a lack of coordination between proposals for reform coming out of MKURABITA and the SPILL process. She expresses concern that "Tanzania is currently undertaking two separate large-scale interventions, one of which is designed to implement the acts, the other to overhaul them."

Implementation of the Village Land Act continued to be slow in the years immediately after SPILL, and certification and registration of both village lands and individual holdings lagged well behind expectations. However, with approval of a World Bank project in December 2005, new financial and technical support began to flow into the program as a part of the Business Environment Strengthening for Tanzania (World Bank 2005). The project earmarked US$30 million of the US$70 million for a land component, but it took nearly two years for implementation to pick up significantly including piloting of systematic adjudication in two of the covered 15 rural districts and land tenure regularization in unplanned settlements in Dar es Salaam and Mwanza. In 2009 the ministry expanded systematic adjudication to two other districts within the 15 targeted rural districts, Namtumbo and Manyoni, using ministry funds.

During 2010 the ministry actively pursued the issuance of CVLs to the estimated 10,000 villages whose boundaries had already been surveyed. As of February 2011, more than 6,600 CVLs had been issued, with more than 3,400 still in process (including preparation of deed plans and printing of the certificates) and yet to be issued. The World Bank provided additional funding to ensure that the remaining CVLs were processed and issued and the remaining villages surveyed and registered by June 2013 (World Bank 2011b). This was critical because villages must have their lands surveyed and certified before the village councils and village land committees can exercise their land management functions or begin mapping and certification of individual holdings.

By 2011 Tanzania had about 0.4 million individual/household titles and 5 percent of its land registered. Just more than 7,000 villages (60 percent) had their land registered. But there is some truth to Pedersen's comment (2010, 17–18) that "the implementation of the Village Land Act has been a process of trial and error for the Ministry of Lands." Excessively heavy dependence on donor funding for geographically limited implementation has resulted in "limiting access to land administrative services for the majority of Tanzanians who live in rural areas" (Pedersen 2010, 1). Knight questions the complexity of the Village Land Act, remarking that although the Act is laudably thorough in providing procedural protections, it "so extensively prescribes these myriad protections, in impenetrable legal language, that they are often lost in the sea of caveats, clauses and exceptions" (Knight 2010, 205–11). There seems to have been a failure to consider the infrastructural needs concerned, and in particular the need for creation of village land registries. Although the Tanzanian approach relies heavily on village level institutions, which should bring about significant economies in the operation of the system, the set-up costs remain substantial. As in Uganda, the Tanzanian programs exceeded available resources and required significant foreign assistance even to pilot.

### Assessment of Decentralization of Land Administration in Tanzania

The decentralization of land administration now under way in Tanzania is a centrally planned and implemented extension of land registry services, closely tied to the program of systematic adjudication and registration of land rights. The decentralization's principal rationale is provision of services to those receiving titles under that program. It involves the creation of community-level land registries linked to the district land registries, where village and household rights are also registered. The new system is thus well integrated vertically, though there appears to have been too limited an emphasis on development of capacity and facilities at the district level, and very little is being done to strengthen capacity in village-level land institutions.

The program is, however, taking place in the context of empowered village-level land management institutions. The relationships between the village land registries and village land committees appear well structured and should make it relatively straightforward for the registries to access the committees' knowledge of landholdings and land transfers in the communities. The power given to villages to manage their land will give them considerable influence over how land administration activities are carried out.

Regarding financial sustainability, it is not clear from the materials consulted for this case study whether this decentralization of land administration is taking place within a well-developed scheme for funding of district and village government activities. The documentation, to a surprising extent, does not address cost of operation issues. The cost of the pilots has been borne by foreign donors and the central government, and the cost of operations down the line does not appear to have received the same attention as in Uganda. It is important that this be addressed with some urgency in discussions of whether to scale up the program. Social sustainability is also an issue, and will, as in Uganda, depend on the extent to which implementation is successful in creating a "culture of registration" strong enough to induce landholders to register transfers and successions. The fact that the village registries link to village land committees bodes well in this regard, and should facilitate efforts to encourage prompt updating of registrations.

## Ethiopia's Experience with Decentralization

Ethiopia's smallholder sector and its institutions are in part the result of the massive land reform carried out by the Derg in 1975, which abolished private property and vested control of lands in local peasant associations. Successor governments have eschewed proposals for empowering smallholders with more robust property rights (Bruce, Hoben, and Rahmato 1994) and reaffirmed the principle of state ownership of land. They have retained prohibitions of sale, mortgage, or exchange and strict limits on leasing. In rural areas, land is managed by the *kebele* (district), a community-level successor institution to the earlier peasant associations created by the Derg. Land is allocated to households, and the landholder has an inheritable right of use, dependent on residence and farming, as well as conditions concerning unspecified "proper" land management practices; failure to observe those practices can result in penalties including loss of the land. General redistributions of landholdings were common after 1991 but have been much less frequent in recent years. They now require approval by a majority of landholders in a given locality.

Although property rights remain much the same as provided for in 1975, land administration arrangements have evolved substantially. Ethiopia is a federal state, with a concurrent power under the constitution. Rural Land Proclamation No. 89/1997 determines the distribution of authority over land. It broadly delegates responsibility for land administration to the ethnically based regional governments, including the ability to develop subsidiary legislation, to assign use rights, and to distribute landholdings. Customary land rights are abolished. Land use rights are inheritable and can in general be leased but not sold or mortgaged. After 1997, several regional governments (Amhara; Tigray; Oromia; and Southern Nations, Nationalities, and People's Region [SNNP]) enacted regional laws consistent with the 1997 proclamation. In addition, major staff transfers were made to the regions from the central ministries that had previously exercised key land competencies. The regional laws recognize the *kebeles'* rights to allocate land and to regulate the use of natural resources, for instance, through the development of community reserves. The *kebele* is now the key local land administration institution (Gebremedhin, Pender, and Tesfaye 2003; Deininger et al. 2008).

The landholding certification program began as a regional initiative in Tigray State in 1998–99. The program was focused on rural land and appears to have been motivated by a desire to reassure landholders—who had suffered numerous land reallocations during the land reforms—that their holdings would now be secure.[4] The region instituted a system of certification in which each holder is provided with a register booklet, with a description of the landholding and the holder's picture. Usually only the male head of household's name is shown on the register book, but in the case of unmarried women, who can own land in their own right, their name is shown. More than 80 percent of the region's population had received new land certificates before the process was interrupted by the war with Eritrea. However, parcels were identified only descriptively, and the records have not been updated to reflect successions or reallocations since then (USAID 2004; Siraj 2006; Deininger et al. 2008; Holden and Tefera 2008).

In 2003 and in 2004, Amhara region launched pilot land certification programs in two rural *kebeles*, Gozamin in East Gojam and Dessie-Zuria in South Wello, with assistance from the Swedish International Development Cooperation Agency (SIDA). The programs have been systematic and participatory. Initial meetings were held at the *woreda* (region) and *kebele* levels. *Woreda*-level boundaries were demarcated first, followed by *kebele* boundaries and those of communal land and service areas. Individual plots were then surveyed using traditional methods and marked with stones (USAID 2004). A local land use and administration committee elected by popular vote for a term of two to three years took responsibility for implementation. Landholders were given a "book of landholdings," issued at the district level, describing the land and their rights over it. For married couples, the names of both spouses were shown on the book, with photographs of both. Copies of the registry book were to be kept at the *kebele* and *woreda* levels. The Oromia and SNNP started their demarcation and certification process later, developing the administrative framework in 2004 and beginning fieldwork in 2005. Overall, first-level rural landholding certificates were issued for 84 percent of holdings in Amhara, 45 percent in Oromia, 51 percent in SNNP, and 99.5 percent in Tigray (Government of Ethiopia 2010, 2). These early land certification programs, typically done without actual survey of parcels, are often referred to collectively as the "Phase 1" programs, and "Phase 2" designates later programs under which parcels are more adequately surveyed. The Phase 1 programs exhibit a significant degree of diversity in their detail, and a full examination of them was beyond the scope of this study.[5]

The enactment of land laws with certification provisions by several states led the federal government to enact a Land Administration Law in 2005 (Proclamation No. 456 of 2005, replacing the 1997 law). The earlier federal law provided for demarcation of land for communal use but had no provision for demarcation and certification of household landholdings; Article 6 of the new law states that rural landholders should be given holding certificates and cadastral maps showing their boundaries and the size of their land. The federal law requires that all state land laws be revised in harmony with it; the federal law supersedes all legislation issued by the state laws in this area of concurrent power. Deininger et al. (2008) suggest, however, that the failure of the 2005 proclamation to specify modifications in greater detail may have left open some scope for bureaucratic discretion at the regional level. In 2010 Amhara and Tigray regions published new laws to harmonize state legislation with the 2005 law, but other states have yet to do so (Rahmato 2009, 72).

In 2006 a United States Agency for International Development (USAID) project to support certification was launched at the federal level, reflecting the national government's appropriation of authority over the program. A five-year USAID Ethiopian Land Tenure and Administration Project (ELTAP) provides assistance to 24 local *woredas* in the four regions. The four regions decided to conduct Phase 2 surveying and certification using handheld Global Positioning System (GPS) equipment to produce geo-referenced and more accurate parcel maps, which are attached to landholding certificates (USAID/Ethiopia 2008). The new program was initiated by a national conference on Standardization of Rural Land Registration and Cadastral Surveying Methodologies on March 20–24, 2006 (Bekure et al. 2010). ELTAP trained several hundred rural land registration clerks and surveyors using private trainers. Second-level cadastral surveying and registration of rural land started in all four regions in 2007, with assistance from SIDA. By 2011 the project had renovated 15 *woreda* and 186 *kebele* offices, developed improved use of handheld GPS units, and demarcated landholdings and registered the rights of 146,824 households to 704,754 parcels of land. Major efforts in public information and judicial training have been carried out.

Important challenges remain for which there are not yet clear government responses, even in the piloting of the Phase 2 work. These include an ongoing debate over the most cost-effective way to achieve greater accuracy in parcel demarcation, lack of a national system of unique parcel identifiers, poor local facilities, weakness in registering subsequent transfers of land, failure to include house plots in the certification process, and uncertainty concerning funding to sustain the system once established (Adenew and Abdi 2005; Deininger et al. 2008; USAID/Ethiopia 2008; Rahmato 2009; Government of Ethiopia 2010). The weakness in registering subsequent transfers is disappointing and suggests a failure in sensitization; the direct involvement of village officials in virtually all transfers and successions should have made this relatively straightforward, but that potential appears not to have been realized.

That said, it seems that some intended impacts of Phase 1 are materializing. Deininger et al. (2008) found that the large majority of beneficiaries perceived certification as likely to increase their incentives to invest in trees, soil and water conservation structures, and sustainable management of common property resources. Most households also expected it to strengthen rental markets and improve women's security of tenure. In Tigray, where the Phase 1 process began earliest, Holden, Deininger, and Ghebru (2007) found that the initial land certification program has had a positive impact on the level of activity in the land rental market. They concluded that the reform reduced transaction costs in that market—though these still remain fairly high—by increasing security and thus making those who wish to lease out land, including female-headed households, more willing to do so. They noted that recent changes in the land proclamation restricting households to leasing out only half of their land may create problems for poor households (including female-headed households) who lack resources to farm their land themselves. Bäckström (2006) reported a reduction of disputes over land following the certification in Tigray, noting that many disagreements over boundaries were adjudicated during the certification process.

In 2010 the government released a concept paper for an ambitious multidonor project to scale up the Phase 2 pilot work. The size of the task remaining is staggering: The concept paper estimates the total number of parcels to be certified at 40.2 million, held by 10.02 million households (Government of Ethiopia 2010, 10). World Bank participation is envisaged, and USAID has designed a follow-on Ethiopia Land Administration Project (ELAP) that would provide continued support in the existing four regions and expand the program to the Afar and Somali regions. ELAP aims to demarcate and certify rights to a further 56,000 households and 280,000 parcels (USAID 2012).

### Assessment of Decentralization of Land Administration in Ethiopia

The programs reviewed here are distinguished from the other countries in this case study by the fact that they began on a state initiative rather than that of the central government. The Phase 1 programs demonstrate the impressive potential of programs that vest implementation in community-level institutions (the *kebeles*) and work with low-cost parcel demarcation methods

(Deininger et al. 2008). Phase 1 was carried out by the regions with active and effective participation by *kebele* institutions, which have replaced traditional authorities. On the other hand, individual communities had no option but to participate. Deininger et al. (2008) suggest that the top-down administrative structure within states and the absence of traditional authorities may have been "propitious" for the implementation of the program.

More recently, the central government has assumed a larger role in these processes, and it is possible that some of the efficiencies in the state-level approach will be lost. The desire to use more sophisticated survey technologies seems to have contributed to this centralization and poses an interesting issue of the relationship between choice of technology and decentralization of land governance. At the community level, however, the *kebeles* can be expected to continue their active engagement, both because they are responsible for maintaining the base land registers and because they have a broader role in land management, including allocation of landholdings, land use planning, and management of commons.

Financially, Phase 2 requires both a substantial central government commitment of funding and major technical assistance and funding from international donor agencies. The cost of operation of the system should be limited by the active roles of community institutions in the longer term, but the cost of maintaining the survey capacity at the *kebele* and *woreda* levels will be significant, and it is not clear in what proportion the central government, state governments, and *kebele* governments will bear those costs.

As elsewhere, social sustainability will be an issue, in terms of whether transfers and successions will be registered promptly by landholders. As in Tanzania, this may be facilitated by the presence of strong land management power at the *kebele* level, and the interactions anticipated between the *kebele* land register and *kebele* land committee. It does need to be borne in mind, however, that productivity payoffs for the program will depend to a great extent upon the government's future policies on property rights. Without stronger rights and their associated incentives, the program's costs may be greater than its benefits. Reports of widespread failure of landholders to register land reassignments and successions in the wake of the Phase I certification are worrying.

## Ghana's Experience with Decentralization

Ghana's land tenure system consists of (1) privately owned land held under statutory tenure; (2) land held under custom, treated by Ghanaian law as a form of private property and including "stool/skin" or throne rights, community rights, and rights of members of those communities; and (3) public or state lands, vested in the President. Customary land predominates, accounting for roughly 80 percent of all land in Ghana, including major urban areas. Land owned under statutory law and documented under a deed registry system are primarily an urban phenomenon, accounting for only about 2 percent of land (Larbi 2011). There is both a deeds registry under the Land Registry Act of 1962 and a largely unimplemented title registration (parcel-based) system under the Land Title Registration Law of 1986. Although the deeds registry deals only with documents for rights under statute law (registration of deeds of transfer, leases, and successions), the title registry registers both statutory and customary rights and transactions concerning those rights (sales, leases, mortgages, and similar transactions, as well as successions under both statutory and customary law) in the areas to which the Title Registration Law has been applied. (As will be seen, however, these areas are extremely limited.) A Lands Commission, which has long administered public lands, was given authority over land surveying and both forms of land registration by the Lands Commission Act of 2008.

Decentralization of land administration in Ghana is proceeding on two fronts. The first initiative is decentralization of government land registration services in connection with systematic expansion of title registration. The registry decentralization builds on other earlier efforts but has received significant impetus from support under the World Bank's Land Administration Project (LAP), which began in 2003. LAP aimed to bring land services closer to those who need them and to implement a "doing business" agenda for reducing the time and costs of accessing those services. Given that most customary rights will not come within the formal system of land administration for many years, the second initiative is focused on upgrading traditional land administration through creation of CLSs. This is intended to improve the quality of records and accessibility of information on landholdings, increase transparency and provide greater accountability in customary land administration, and inform policy development (Toulmin, Brown, and Crook 2004). The intention of this program "pivoted on equity grounds: indirectly alleviating poverty by ensuring that entry barriers to securing title to land claims by small land owners are assured" (Antwi 2006, 4–5).

The registry decentralization has progressed satisfactorily. The midterm report for the project indicates that the objective was to have deed registries established in four regional capitals, and one-stop service centers established in three regions (Government of Ghana 2006). By 2010 deed registries existed in eight regional capitals, compared to two at the outset of the project. Decentralization and reforms in procedures were said to have resulted in the reduction in the time it takes to register a deed from six months to one to two months, and the time needed to transfer a registered title from 36 days to 6 days (Larbi 2011; World Bank 2011a). The systematic land registration pilots have mapped and inventoried rights for about 15,000 urban parcels but so far only about 75 titles have been issued (Larbi 2011). A further Bank project (LAP-2) will provide continued support to strengthen the decentralized offices, including their automation of business procedures (World Bank 2011a). The one-stop shop concept seems not to figure in LAP-2, because its efforts focus more on building capacity in district registries.

Organizationally, the District Land Offices would be part of the Land Commission (LC), report to the Regional Land Commission (RLC), receive financial support from the LC, and follow a staffing pattern determined by the RLC. The District Assembly is expected to provide office space and some support. Fees would be collected by the land office for receiving and registering records and for providing copies of searches for private sector and individual clients. A memorandum of understanding between the LC and the district would address respective roles, coordination mechanisms, exchanges of information and records, input and cost contributions, performance management, and linkages with the traditional authorities (World Bank, Government of Ghana, and Canadian International Development Agency 2010).

In 2007 the Millennium Challenge Corporation initiated a five-year program of support of both decentralization and pilot systematic title registration, operated within the LAP framework. A systematic registration pilot has been carried out in the customary area of Awutu Senya, in the south, and a local land registry with a Continually Operating Reference Station capability was established there, operated by the LAP. The pilot has surveyed more than 3,800 hectares, but only 570 title certificates (18 percent of the potential titles) have been issued. The initial definition of the adjudication area used physical features that cut through the middle of local communities, with predictable results (Karikari and Barthel 2011). However, the pilot has had numerous notable successes: consensus achieved on the nature of customary rights to be registered; successful promotion of written leases for customary tenants, allowing their holdings to be registered; and registration of a substantial number of women landholders. A second pilot area has been identified in the north, at Savelugu-Nanton, with a planned adjudication area of 2,600 hectares (Karikari and Barthel 2011).

Implementation of the CLS program began with three existing CLSs, established by traditional authorities prior to the project. A further three pilots were initially established in areas with no existing CLSs. All pilots were supplied with office equipment including computers. Facilitators were provided to initiate activities. Attention focused on the following themes: (1) urban customary land ownership and transactions, (2) information capture and dissemination, (3) rural customary land ownership and transactions, (4) economics and general estate management of CLSs, (5) legal environment and CLSs, and (6) land rights dispute resolution. Several concerns emerged in the pilots, including complaints that chiefs were allocating land to people from outside the community. CLSs lack authority over residential lands and land disputes, and many have no bank accounts (Antwi 2006). Misgivings persisted about the potential of the CLSs. Antwi (2006, 5) warned that if the issues of fairness, transparency, and accountability could not be effectively addressed by the program, "occupiers of stools/skins may use enhanced and equipped CLS to further tendencies of dispossessing their subjects of lands." Ubink and Quan (2008, 198) expressed concern that the establishment of CLSs risks entrenching unaccountable land management. A discussion continued within the LAP and the LC as to whether the chiefs should be absorbed into the formal system of land administration, and whether it was time to provide a statutory basis for the CLS; up to that point, each CLS was based on an memorandum of agreement between the government and the chief (Bruce 2006b).

The World Bank is continuing its support for the CLS program and reports the LAP's achievements as 38 CLSs established, with an estimated 58,000 land records compiled (World Bank, Government of Ghana, and Canadian International Development Agency 2010). In selected CLS areas, the project will support piloting of a systematic process of demarcating and documenting rights to all parcels, beginning with the large areas of land owned by chiefdoms (Burgi 2009; World Bank et al. 2010; World Bank 2011a). This follows the general direction suggested by a 2009 University of New Brunswick report (Burgi 2009), which recommended developing the CLSs as local land registries and eventually linking them into the national land registration system (World Bank et al. 2010).

The most recent draft of a comprehensive Lands Act (Draft 3, 2011) makes it clear where the government is headed. Articles 220–23 set out a legal framework for the CLSs, requiring "a customary land owning group" to establish a CLS for the management of its land; this includes recording the rights and interests in land, keeping and maintaining accurate and up-to-date records of land transactions, and settling land disputes through mediation. The CLSs are to determine their own structure and staffing, appointing staff themselves. The Regional or District Lands Officer is given supervisory authority over the CLSs to ensure that they comply with their mandates and is empowered to "give directions to any officer of a CLS as to the proper performance of duties, and that officer shall be under a duty to comply with any such directions." Funding for the CLSs are to come from fees they charge and from a number of existing central government revenue sources, but the proportions are not specified. Based on the draft act, it would appear that the direction charted by the government for the CLSs lies toward the "service provider" role, and integration into the national system of land administration. It does not refer at all to traditional authorities, and it appears that the CLSs will function alongside those authorities, providing them and their subjects with services.

### Assessment of Decentralization of Land Administration in Ghana

Decentralization of land administration in Ghana on both the registry and CLS tracks have been implemented as a central government initiative, in conjunction with modest piloting of systematic land title registration. Regional and district registries have been the principal beneficiaries. The connection between their establishment and the work on the CLS track has become clearer in the last few years; rather than developing the CLSs within the traditional land governance framework, the government plans to transform them into the lowest level of civil land administration, as service units run by the government for the use of those authorities and their subjects.

The end result of this experiment would be decentralization to an ambitiously local level, to civil rather than traditional authorities. Although traditional authorities retain their ownership and control of customary lands, they appear to have no formal role in relation to the CLSs. They seem to be cast in the role of clients, as users of the system. This appears out of sync with local power realities, especially in the more powerful chiefdoms. The net result is a decentralization that is more deconcentration than devolution.

Agricultural Land Redistribution and Land Administration in Sub-Saharan Africa
http://dx.doi.org/10.1596/978-1-4648-0188-4

Regarding sustainability, the funding issues around these new local land administration institutions are critical. For the time being, donor funds are assisting with these issues and perhaps masking their severity. The survey capacity envisaged to maintain the registry system at the district level will be expensive to maintain. Districts and regions will have to negotiate with the central government the division of funding needed to support new local registries. Without new funding, these negotiations could be very contentious. There is no indication that there is a politically viable strategy for addressing these funding issues.

As with the other countries covered in this case study, sustainability of the new system will also depend on whether landholders appreciate the creation of records of land rights and whether they are willing to actively participate in updating the system. The CLSs seem destined to be developed outside the control of traditional authorities, who are still important opinion leaders in their communities; this may create tensions and make it more difficult to achieve sustainability.

## Comparisons and Lessons Learned

The land policy contexts of the decentralization processes compared here are somewhat different. Ghana and Uganda have strong private property systems. In their cases, the objectives of the extension of a title registration system through systematic adjudication and registration are both enhanced security of land tenure and more efficient and trustworthy functioning of land markets. Both countries have extensive areas under legally recognized customary land tenure, and traditional institutions still play important land roles at the grassroots level. Their registration programs formalize those customary rights. Harmonization of statutory and customary rights and institutions is thus an important consideration in their programs. In Ethiopia and Tanzania, although the formalization and service provision motivation is important, land markets are restricted by law, and land use planning is a much stronger motivation than in Ghana and Uganda. Control of land use and land distribution are important objectives. Both Ethiopia and Tanzania earlier broke the hold of traditional authorities over land and replaced them with civil community-level institutions. Ethiopia and Tanzania do not recognize customary land rights as such, but do recognize and protect possession. In their registration programs, both countries formalize landholders as holders of statutory rights, not customary rights.

Some key elements in the four country's programs are set out in Table 3.1; the most important differences in the nature of their decentralization programs are elaborated in the text that follows.

In both Uganda and Ghana, decentralization involves the reform and rehabilitation of weak land registration systems and their extension to more local levels. Systematic demarcation and registration is part of that process, providing the database required for effective civil land administration. A strong emphasis is put on using the most modern cadastral methods. The objective of decentralization is not to replace customary rights but to improve the administration of lands

**Table 3.1 Key Elements of Land Administration Decentralization Programs**

| | Ghana | Uganda | Ethiopia | Tanzania |
|---|---|---|---|---|
| Tenure policy and legal context | Private ownership and customary rights recognized and registrable. Active land markets. | Private ownership and customary rights recognized and registrable. Active land markets. | Statutory rights less than ownership recognized and registrable. Land marketability limited. | Statutory rights less than ownership recognized, and registrable. Land marketability limited. |
| Roles decentralized and institutions enabled | Registration and update of records of land rights to local government level. | Registration and update of records of land rights to local government level. | Registration and update of records of land rights to local government and community level. | Registration and update of records of land rights to local government and community level. |
| Deconcentration or devolution of land administration functions | Deconcentration: extension of central government land administration system. | Deconcentration: extension of central government land administration system. | Deconcentration: extension of central government land administration system. | Deconcentration: extension of central government land administration system. |
| Interaction with local land management institutions | New land administration capacity created outside traditional authorities. Unclear links to new local land management institutions. | New land administration capacity created outside traditional authorities. Unclear links to new local land management institutions. | New land administration capacity created in local land management institutions, empowering them. | New land administration capacity created in local land management institutions, empowering them. |
| Financial sustainability | Cost sharing unclear. No provision for retention of revenues. | Cost sharing unclear. No provision for retention of revenues. | Cost sharing unclear. No provision for retention of revenues. | Cost sharing unclear. No provision for retention of revenues. |
| Social sustainability | Unclear connections to local land management authorities could limit sustainability. | Unclear connections to local land management authorities could limit sustainability. | Potential increased by decentralizing land administration and management functions to same local institution. | Potential increased by decentralizing land administration and management functions to same local institution. |

under custom. In both Uganda and Ghana, the roles of local traditional and civil authorities seem to be changing. In Uganda, land policy and law call for gradual replacement of traditional authorities by local civil land governance institutions, but the actual situation is very mixed. The decentralization program does not address this directly and has done little to strengthen the new local civil land governance institutions. The land administration system is being extended into the rural areas in a service-provision mode, alongside but not well integrated with those local land governance institutions. In Ghana, the same emphasis is found on decentralization of registry offices to provide better documentation of customary land rights, and no suggestion that customary rights are to be altered. CLSs have been established by the government to facilitate traditional land administration. It now seems, however, that the CLSs are to become the bottom rung of the civil land administration system. As in Uganda, they would then function as providers of land administration services to customary landholders, including the traditional authorities, whose land governance roles, for the time being at least, are largely unchanged. In time, however, the databases created in the local land registries can provide the government with the information it needs to take over more direct administration of customary land, and this may presage a decline in the role of traditional authorities. This should make proposed legal provisions on Ghana's CLSs contentious.

In Ethiopia the strong civil local authorities at the *kebele* and *woreda* levels have been given a very considerable role in the initial identification of right holders and their holdings. In Tanzania, setting up the land administration system at the local level has always been seen as a central government function, whereas in Ethiopia it was initiated at the regional level and then taken over by the central government. In both countries there is substantial local participation in implementation by community-level institutions. The potential for such participation was increased by the presence of civil community governance structures closely linked into the regional and national systems of territorial governance. In both countries, land registers will be maintained by these local governance structures, and this should facilitate keeping up-to-date registry information. These local institutions have important land use planning and allocation roles. They are close enough to local land users to know when transfers of land take place and are well enough integrated into the overall national system of land governance to be held accountable for ensuring that the necessary formalities are observed and for transferring information upward within the system. There is some question, however, of whether these potentials are being realized, at least in Ethiopia.

In all four countries, it is clear that the land registry system itself will eventually operate on a far more decentralized basis. As it relates to land administration functions, this decentralization is a deconcentration in all four countries, extending state knowledge and control of land. The decentralization does, however, have the potential to enhance community-level land management where land management functions are decentralized as well, to the same institutions. This is the case in Ethiopia and Tanzania, so decentralization puts new information and tools for land management in the hands of their local institutions. Decentralization of land administration should thus empower them in their land management roles. In Uganda and Ghana, however, this connection does not exist in the same fashion, or is not so clear, so decentralization of land administration may not empower local land institutions in the same fashion.

Because of the levels of survey technology being employed, the systems being created will be fairly expensive to maintain. It is unclear how far the costs of operating these systems will be assumed by central or more local levels of government. African governments have been reluctant to impose land taxes, and a too-heavy reliance on fees for services will drive land users out of the system and into more informal arrangements. A clear division of responsibilities for funding such systems is essential, and the manner in which the responsibility is allocated may be an important element in their sustainability. The allocation could influence both perceptions of "ownership" and the relative influence of different levels of government on the operations of these systems.

The sustainability of the decentralized land administration in these four countries will also depend upon landholders' buy-in. The records created at great expense will go out of date soon unless land users are motivated to come forward to register transfers and successions. The solution lies in part in serious public education and sensitization and prioritization of the creation of functional registry offices contemporary with, rather than years after, the initial registrations. But it will also depend on whether landholders experience greater tenure security. This is an issue in Ethiopia and Tanzania, where there are important legal limits on land markets and use of land as collateral for loans. Ironically, in Ethiopia the history of reallocations may generate a stronger appreciation of any increment in security of tenure provided by certification and generate a stronger willingness for landholders to support the system's maintenance.

It is worth noting that donors in Ethiopia and Tanzania have not been deterred by the fact that the property rights concerned are use rights rather than ownership rights. Those rights have little potential as security for loans. In Ethiopia they are still subject to reallocation under certain conditions, and can be taken if left idle for three years. This potentially undermines the traditional economic case for investment in land administration, which leans heavily on lowering risk in markets and facilitating use of land to secure loans. Yet the donors involved seem not to be concerned; no conditionality requiring law reform has been imposed. The practice in the World Bank has been to move away from such conditionalities, because they are often not effective (Bruce 2006a, 23). Instead, reliance is placed on persuasion during design and implementation of the project to convince the government of the need for policy and law reforms. This is a calculated gamble. If such reforms are not forthcoming, investments in land administration may not show economic rates of return that are competitive with other development programs. If legal reforms do not materialize within the project term, it may be that the documentation and certification of land holdings—stressing as they do the importance of the rights involved—will in time create rising expectations of and demand for stronger property rights.

Agricultural Land Redistribution and Land Administration in Sub-Saharan Africa
http://dx.doi.org/10.1596/978-1-4648-0188-4

This case study reveals some factors that condition the choices being made regarding decentralization of land administration in Africa, such as the following:

- Decentralization of land administration happens within more general patterns of decentralization of government and public services, which creates opportunities and constraints. In particular, these larger programs provide a framework for cost sharing by different levels of government. Because that framework is independent of land administration structures, it is difficult to find information regarding it in LAP documentation, or indeed any indication that fiscal sustainability of the new systems has been seriously considered.

- Decentralization to the community level can be greatly facilitated if there are already in existence community institutions capable of undertaking that task. Where traditional authorities still handle most local land governance, this may or may not be feasible; it will depend on a variety of factors, including their receptivity and probity. If this is not feasible, it may be necessary to build a land administration competence in local government, a daunting task. This is not an either/or choice; in some countries not covered in this case study, such as Botswana and Niger, hybrid local land committees have included both traditional and civil authorities.

- Decentralization of land administration tasks tends to be a deconcentration of central government authority, reflecting in part the desire to facilitate the functioning of national land markets; on the other hand, when the land administration function is decentralized to local institutions with important land management roles, that decentralization can empower them in their land management roles.

- Land administration systems established through systematic survey and adjudication of rights have often experienced problems with sustainability because of failure of landholders to register transfers and successions. Sustainability may be set back if local authorities who deal with land management on a daily basis feel shut out from or undermined by the creation of local registries unconnected with them. Clarifying the relationship between registries and the most local levels of land governance, whether civil or traditional, will be critical to sustainability.

- Initial decentralization of any sophisticated land administration machinery likely requires a strong central government lead and assistance to communities. A regional or district lead may suffice for very simple systems, but where sophisticated technologies are involved, that lead will usually need to come from the central government. There is thus an important link between decentralization and the choice of survey and other technologies.

- There are important roles for community institutions in the maintenance and operation of the decentralized system, even where the central government takes a strong lead, especially in initial identification of holdings and right holders. This can extend to keeping primary registers, where these can be maintained manually. This has a potential for keeping the records up-to-date, though the task of creating a "culture of registration," in which community members understand that updating is in their best interest, still remains.

- The institutional framework for decentralized land administration should be planned conservatively, with a clear sense of the magnitude of costs of long-term maintenance of the system and how funds will be made available for them. The fact that donor funding is available for the creation of these systems should not obscure the fact that maintenance and operational costs will ultimately need to be met from domestic resources, nor should the availability of donor funding be allowed to encourage governments to opt for technologies that will be too expensive to maintain in the long run.

- Laws providing for that institutional framework should not attempt to specify in detail the technologies and staffing concerned. Technologies change rapidly, and staffing will depend on the skills available and needed locally. Nor should the law require registries at a particular administration level at each and every instance; shared use of a registry by two or more administrative units may be sensible in the early development of the institutions. Legally imposed rigidity in this respect should be avoided.

- In light of the growing international demand for land, there is new urgency to recognize and document the rights of rural people. The Ethiopian Phase I approach, with its very rough parcel identification, is the only approach among the four considered here that can respond to this massive need inexpensively and quickly. On a household landholding level, Ethiopia's program is comparable to what has been done on a community landholding basis in Mozambique.

This case study also raises some questions that deserve consideration:

- The programs considered here all aspire to provide the same levels of survey precision and rights throughout their respective nations. But do the more remote areas really need the same level of recording as those areas that are more accessible and that have more heavily sought after land? Although there may be a political impetus to provide the same security of tenure to all, would it not be more cost effective to design programs that would, for example in the case of Ethiopia, leave some communities in Phase 1 longer, with scaling up to Phase 2 only when there is a real need for a greater level of precision?

- Much of the return to the major investment in systematic creation of land administration systems and their decentralization to local levels is anticipated to come from making land markets more trustworthy and user-friendly. In both Ethiopia and Tanzania, where land transactions are legally limited in significant ways, can the economic case be made for the investment? The programs can clearly serve security of tenure ends, but is this enough to justify the initial investment? Will it be enough to justify maintenance costs? If not, what are the implications for sustainability of these systems? Or will the new land administration facilities stimulate demand for stronger guarantees of property rights and marketability of land rights?

## Notes

1. Numerous useful comparative reports are available on decentralization of land administration and related issues in Africa, each with its own orientation. See, e.g., Augustinus (2003), Wily (2003a), and Bruce and Knox (2009). For francophone Africa, see Rochegude (2002) and Lavigne-Delville (2000, 2010).
2. Exchange rate as of December 31, 2013.
3. The Land Tribunals stopped operating around 2007 because of lack of funding after they were transferred from the Ministry of Lands to the Ministry of Justice.
4. It should be noted that land rights are not generally transferable, but change hands (officially, at least) through reassignment by village-level committees, principally in the inheritance context. While very limited leasing is allowed, those leases are not required to be registered.
5. See Abebe (2006) for a thorough treatment of this topic.

## References

Abebe, S. 2006. "Land Registration System in Ethiopia; Comparative Analysis of Amhara, Oromia, SNNP and Tigray Regional States." In *Standardization of Rural Land Registration and Cadastral Methodologies; Experiences in Ethiopia, Proceedings of a National Conference*, edited by S. Bekure, G. Abegaz, L. Frej, and S. Abebe. Addis Ababa: Ethiopia—Strengthening Land Tenure and Administration Program (ELTAP).

Adenew, B., and F. Abdi. 2005. *Land Registration in Amhara Region, Ethiopia*. Research Report 3, IIED Securing Land Rights in Africa, London.

Antwi, Y. A. 2006. "Strengthening Customary Land Administration: A DFID/World Bank Sponsored Project in Ghana." Paper prepared for Promoting Land Administration and Good Governance, 5th FIG Regional Conference, Accra, Ghana, March 8–11.

Augustinus, C. 2003. "Comparative Analysis of Land Administration Systems: African Review with Special Reference to Mozambique, Uganda, Namibia, Ghana, South Africa." World Bank, Nairobi.

Bäckström, L. 2006. "Look at Ethiopia! A Simplified and Result Oriented Development and Implementation of a Low Cost Land Administration System." Paper prepared for the XXIII FIG Congress "Shaping the Change," Munich, Germany, October 8–13.

Bekure, S., G. Abegaz, L. Frej, and S. Abebe, eds. 2010. "Standardization of Rural Land Registration and Cadastral Methodologies; Experiences in Ethiopia." Proceedings of a National Conference, Ethiopia—Strengthening Land Tenure and Administration Program (ELTAP), Addis Ababa.

Bruce, J. W. 2006a. "Reform of Land Law in the Context of World Bank Lending." In *Land Law Reform: Achieving Development Policy Objectives*, edited by J. W. Bruce, R. Giovarelli, L. Rolfes Jr., D. Bledsoe, and R. Mitchell, 11–65. Washington, DC: Legal Vice-Presidency, World Bank.

———. 2006b. *Land Administration Project (Ghana), Consultancy Service on Legal and Institutional Issues*. Report prepared for the DFID, London.

Bruce, J. W., A. Hoben, and D. Rahmato. 1994. *After the Derg: An Assessment of Rural Land Tenure Issues in Ethiopia*. Land Tenure Center, University of Wisconsin–Madison.

Bruce, J. W., and A. Knox. 2009. "Structures and Stratagems: Decentralization of Authority over Land in Africa." *World Development* (Special Issue on the Limits of State-Led Land Reform) 37 (8): 1360–69.

Bruce, J., and S. E. Mighot-Adholla, eds. 1994. *Searching for Land Tenure Security in Africa*. New York: Kendall/Hunt Publishing Company.

Burgi, J. 2009. *Survey Report on Customary Land Secretariats in Ghana*. Report by the Centre for Property Studies/Terradigm, University of New Brunswick.

Burns, T. 2007. "Land Administration Reform: Indicators of Success, Future Challenges." Agriculture and Rural Development Discussion Paper 37, World Bank, Washington, DC.

Byamugisha, F. F. K. 2013. *Securing Africa's Land for Shared Prosperity: A Program to Scale Up Reforms and Investments*. Africa Development Forum Series. Washington, DC: World Bank.

Deininger, K., D. Ayalew Ali, S. Holden, and J. Zevenbergen. 2008. "Rural Land Certification in Ethiopia: Process, Initial Impact, and Implications for Other African Countries." *World Development* 36: 1786–812.

Gebremedhin, B., J. Pender, and G. Tesfaye. 2003. "Community Natural Resource Management: The Case of Woodlots in Northern Ethiopia." *Environment and Development Economics* 8 (1): 129–48.

Government of Ethiopia, Ministry of Agriculture and Rural Development. 2010. "Concept Note on the Design and Implementation of Ethiopia Land Administration and Land Use Development Project (ELALUDEP)." Ministry of Agriculture and Rural Development, Addis Ababa.

Government of Ghana, Land Administration Project Unit, Ministry of Lands, Forestry and Mines. 2006. "Land Administration Project Mid-Term Review. Progress Report October 2003–June 2006 and Proposals for Restructuring the Project." Ministry of Lands, Forestry and Mines, Accra.

Government of Tanzania, Ministry of Lands, Housing and Settlement Development. 2006. "Private Sector Competitiveness Project: Component, Sub-component B. Land Reform Project Implementation Manual." Ministry of Lands, Housing and Settlement Development, Dar es Salaam.

Government of Tanzania, Ministry of Lands, Housing and Urban Development. 1994. *Report of the Presidential Commission of Inquiry into Land Matters*, vol. I. Uppsala, Sweden: Scandinavian Institute of African Studies.

Government of Uganda, Ministry of Lands, Housing and Urban Development. 2001. "Land Sector Strategic Plan 2001–2011: Utilizing Uganda's Land Resources for Sustainable Development." Ministry of Land, Housing and Urban Development, Kampala.

Holden, S. T., K. Deininger, and H. Ghebru. 2007. "Impact of Land Certification on Land Rental Market Participation in Tigray Region, Northern Ethiopia." Paper presented at the Nordic Development Economics Conference, Copenhagen, June 18–19. MPRA Munich Personal RePEc Archive, http://mpra.ub.uni-muenchen .de/5211/.

Holden, S., and T. Tefera. 2008. *From Being Property of Men to Becoming Equal Owners? Early Impacts of Land Registration and Certification on Women in Southern Ethiopia.* Research report for UNHABITAT, Shelter Division, Nairobi.

Hunt, D. 2004. "Unintended Consequences of Land Rights Reform: The Case of the 1998 Uganda Land Act." *Development Policy Review* 22 (2): 173–91.

Instituto Liberdad y Democracia. 2005. "Volume III: The Legal Economy: Its Institutions and Costs." Unpublished MKURABITA document, Dar es Salaam.

Karikari, I., and K. Barthel. 2011. "Contributions in the Land Sector through the Millennium Development Authority's Agriculture Project in Ghana: Strategic and Technical Progress and Lessons." Paper presented at Annual World Bank Conference on Land and Poverty, Washington, DC, April 18–20.

Knight, R. 2010. "Statutory Recognition of Customary Land Rights in Africa: An Investigation into Best Practices for Lawmaking and Implementation." FAO Legislative Study 15, FAO, Rome.

Kosyando, O. M. L. 2007. "MKURABITA and the Implementation of the Village Land Law—Act No 5 of 1999." TAPHGO, Arusha, Tanzania. http://www.tnrf.org/files /E-INFO_TAPHGO_report_on_MKURABITA_Handeni_land_registration_0.pdf.

———. 2008. "A Participation Report of MKURABITA's Land Titling Pilot Project in Bagamoyo District, Coast Region, Tanzania." September 2007–February 2008, TAPHGO, Arusha, Tanzania.

Larbi, O. (Commissioner of Lands). 2011. "Ghana's LAP: Accomplishments, Impacts, and the Way Ahead CEO." Paper presented at the Annual World Bank Conference on Land and Poverty, April 18–20, Washington, DC.

Lavigne-Delville, P. 2000. "Harmonising Formal Law and Customary Land Rights in French-Speaking Africa." In *Evolving Land Rights, Policy and Tenure in Africa*, edited by C. Toulmin and J. Quan, 97–122. London: DFID/IIED/NRI.

———. 2010. "Registering and Administering Customary Land Rights: Can We Deal with Complexity?" In *Innovations in Land Rights Recognition, Administration, and Governance*, edited by K. Deininger, C. Augustinus, S. Enemark, and P. Munro-Faure, 24–42. Washington, DC: World Bank.

McAuslan, P. 2003. *Bringing the Law Back In: Essays in Land, Law and Development.* Ashgate, U.K.: Aldershot.

Msangi, A. (Commissioner of Lands). 2005. "Overview of the Status of Implementation of the 1999 Land Acts." In *Report on the Proceedings of the Symposium on the Implementation of the 1999 Land Acts.* Dar es Salaam, Tanzania.

NORAD, The United Republic of Tanzania URT, The President's Office, and J. Claussen. 2008. "Annual Review of the Property and Business Formalisation Programme (RBFP) in Tanzania." NORAD, Oslo.

Okidi, J. A., and M. Guloba. 2006. "Decentralization and Development. Emerging Lessons from Uganda's Experience." Occasional Paper 31, Economic Policy Research Center, Kampala.

Palmer, R. 1999. "The Tanzanian Land Acts, 1999: An Analysis of the Analyses." Oxfam GB, London.

Pedersen, R. H. 2010. "Tanzania's Land Law Reform; the Implementation Challenge." DIIS Working Paper 37, Danish Institute of International Studies, Copenhagen.

Rahmato, D. 2009. "Land Rights and Tenure Security: Rural Land Registration in Ethiopia." In *Legalizing Land Rights. Local Practices, State Responses, and Tenure Security in Africa, Asia and Latin America*, edited by J. M. Ubink, A. I. Hoekema, and W. J. Assies. Leiden: Leiden University Press.

Ribot, J. C. 2001. "Local Actors, Powers and Accountability in African Decentralization: A Review of Key Issues." Paper prepared for IDRC, Canada, Assessment of Social Policy Reforms Initiative, World Resources Institute, Washington, DC.

Rochegude, A. 2002. "Foncier et décentralisation. Réconcilier la légalité et la légitimité des pouvoirs domaniaux et fonciers." *Cahiers d'Anthropologie du Droit* 15–43.

Siraj, A. 2006. "Options for Updating Land Records: The Case of Tigray Region." In *Standardization of Rural Land Registration and Cadastral Methodologies: Experiences in Ethiopia. Proceedings of a National Conference*, edited by S. Bekure, G. Abegaz, L. Frej, and S. Abebe. Addis Ababa: Ethiopia-Strengthening Land Tenure and Administration Program (ELTAP).

Toulmin, C., D. Brown, and R. Crook. 2004. "Project Memorandum: Ghana Land Administration Project, Institutional Reform & Development: Strengthening Customary Land Administration." DFID-Ghana, Accra.

Ubink, J. M., and J. F. Quan. 2008. "How to Combine Tradition and Modernity? Regulating Customary Land Management in Ghana." *Land Use Policy* 25 (2): 198–213.

USAID. 2004. *Ethiopia Land Policy and Administration Assessment; Final Report with Appendices*. ARD, Burlington, VT.

———. 2012. "Ethiopia-Strengthening Land Administration Program." ELAP News.

USAID/Ethiopia and Ministry of Agriculture and Rural Development. 2008. "Strengthening Land Tenure and Administration Program. Performance Monitoring Report, Cumulative Summary, August 2005–June 2008." ARD, Burlington, VT.

Wily, L. A. 2003a. *Governance and Land Relations: A Review of Decentralization of Land Administration and Management in Africa*. London: IIED.

———. 2003b. "Community-Based Land Tenure Management. Questions and Answers about Tanzania's New Village Land Act, 1999." Drylands Issue Paper E120, IIED, London.

World Bank. 2005. "Tanzania Private Sector Competitiveness Project." Project Appraisal Document, World Bank, Washington, DC.

———. 2008a. "Uganda Second Private Sector Competitiveness Project—Land Component, World Bank 7th Implementation Support Mission (Mid-term Review) Aide Memoir." World Bank, Washington, DC.

———. 2008b. "Land Component. Mid-Term Implementation Review Report. Private Sector Competitiveness Project II." World Bank, Washington, DC.

———. 2011a. "Project Appraisal Document on a Proposed Credit in the Amount of SDR 32.1 Million (US $50 Million Equivalent) to the Republic of Ghana for a Land Administration Project 2." World Bank, Washington, DC.

———. 2011b. "Tanzania–Land Component of the Private Sector Competitiveness Project. Findings of World Bank Mission–March 2 to 4, 2011." World Bank, Washington, DC.

————. 2013. "Uganda Competitiveness and Enterprise Development Project." Project Appraisal Document, World Bank, Washington, DC.

World Bank, Government of Ghana, and Canadian International Development Agency. 2010. "LAP II Appraisal on Land Registration and Related Activities." World Bank, Washington, DC.

# CHAPTER 4

# Land Administration Challenges in Postconflict States in Sub-Saharan Africa: Lessons from Rwanda and Liberia

John Bruce

If countries emerging from conflict are to begin the process of economic recovery, resettle refugees and displaced people, and prevent land grabbing by the powerful, they will have to deal with land rights. And they have to do this while avoiding further social tensions, injustice or secondary conflicts.

—BRUCE 2009

## Postconflict Challenges to Land Administration

This case study looks at the experiences of Rwanda and Liberia to identify lessons for reconstituting effective land administration systems in postconflict situations. Their experiences are illuminating in many respects, and the importance of "getting land right" after their conflicts is well summed up in a statement heard in both places: "If we go to war again, it will be over land."

Land, of course, plays a variety of roles in conflict, in what can be thought of as a conflict cycle: It can be a key *cause* of the conflict; it can be a factor in *maintaining the conflict*, as contending factions struggle over land to control inhabitants and high-value resources that can be used to sustain conflict; and it can be a key factor *after* the conflict, because preconflict land problems still need to be addressed, because they have been transformed and reconfigured by the conflict but remain a threat to peace, or because the conflict itself has created land problems that did not previously exist. In most postconflict situations, new contention over land is caused by the displacement of populations during conflict and restitution claims of returning refugees to be addressed. However, regardless of the specific context, tensions over land may threaten to rekindle violent conflict, fueled by deep passions of injustice and the threat to livelihoods, and exacerbated by questions of identity and class (Bruce 2009; Leckie and Huggins 2011).

After a prolonged serious conflict or civil war, land governance—not to mention governance generally—is often in a shambles. The severity of the situation will vary depending upon the length and intensity of the conflict and whether it has been localized or general. Box 4.1 sets out a disheartening (fictitious) scenario that will be familiar to those who have worked in countries emerging from long periods of conflict.

Land administration systems that are in such a parlous state need urgent attention, and this case study highlights how important concerted and rapid support can be. In the face of such a chaotic situation, it is also easy either to focus on issues of policy while neglecting to rebuild implementation capacity, or to focus on rebuilding the land administration system without regard to the underlying sociology and economics of the land in question in a particular country. It is important to look fundamentally at policy issues *before or at least along with* any program to reform or reconstitute the land administration system. This case study focuses on rebuilding effective land administration systems, but this important point should not be overlooked.

Two sets of land administration needs must be addressed in a postconflict situation. There are short-term needs, such as resolving displacement-related disputes over land and resettling refugees. This is essentially "fire-fighting," getting

---

### Box 4.1  Land Administration Postconflict Year 1

After 20 years of civil war, the offices of the Land Ministry sit empty except for a few staff who wander by occasionally, wondering if something may be happening. The offices have been looted, survey and other equipment stolen or smashed, and copper wire torn out of the walls. Only a few of the trained staff from a generation ago are still around. For years, salaries have been paid only sporadically, if at all. Most staffers have other, more remunerative unofficial work, and if they are in the office much, it is to use the facilities for that work. In these circumstances, both management and work ethics have crumbled. Public services are rendered on a largely "user-pays" basis, with service providers pocketing the payment. Many of the records of rights to land and land disputes so essential to effective land administration may have been lost. Land registries may have been burned to the ground. If the land records have survived, they may have been badly damaged. Pages from them may be found in the local market, used as wrapping materials in which children sell peanuts. Deed records may be piled on the floors of deserted offices, their shelves stolen for scrap metal, the documents exposed to the elements in rooms whose windows are long gone. Copies of statute books cannot be found. The effective rule-of-law vacuum invites the powerful and savvy to prey upon the weak. Lost and damaged land records facilitate fraud and simple illegal appropriation of the land of others. Continuing uncontrolled competition over land in such a governance vacuum poses a danger to peace-building processes and threatens to lead the country back into violence. The courts are empty, with few judges still present.

*Source:* Adapted from Bruce 2009.

people back onto the land and restoring livelihoods with a minimum of conflict. Badly planned resettlements have proved to be a source of continuing contention over land. In such situations, where public land administrations are very likely to have no presence at all in the field, local and customary structures may play an essential role and require due recognition in any future settlement. This is the case in the countries examined here and is common in postconflict contexts elsewhere in Africa, for example, in Mozambique (Tanner 2002).

Careful planning of even short-term measures is essential because short-term measures that appear expedient at the time can take on a permanent character. If they are not well thought through, they can create a new source of future conflict as longer-term, "permanent" solutions are put in place. Also, it is not effective or appropriate for humanitarian agencies to get stuck in the fire-fighting mode and neglect national land administration institutions. If this happens, as it did in Liberia, frustration will grow in national institutions as they watch outsiders work their "patch" while they receive little support to reassume their mandates.

Although an effective and informed short-term response is critical, this case study focuses on the longer-term task of rebuilding land administration, restoring government capacity so that it can reassert effective control of its land sector. Rebuilding what existed before may not suffice: New institutions and laws may be needed. This is the work of several years or more, and it is not something that the international community can do for postconflict states. Land system reforms will not succeed without country ownership and commitment, and for these to exist, the government must make complex choices involved in designing those initiatives. In the immediate postconflict period, when "fire-fighting" holds center stage, there will be a need for assessments to scope out land issues and determine needs. As soon as possible, work must begin in rebuilding both management and technical capacities in land sector institutions. Only when land sector agencies have been restored to some degree can they begin to move into more systematic policy making and law reforms.

Rwanda and Liberia provide useful case studies. In both countries land issues quickly came to the fore of postconflict national concerns, and in both countries, the government appreciated the severity of the issues concerned. Donors made funding available to address them, if somewhat belatedly. The two countries took rather different tracks in developing strategies and implementing them. Rwanda moved relatively rapidly in a radical reform, while Liberia's approach was more considered and its direction is not yet clear. After reviewing their experiences, this case study suggests some lessons learned for reestablishing systems of land administration and embarking on needed reforms in a postconflict context.

## Rwanda's Postconflict Land Administration

The civil war and genocide in Rwanda created major challenges for postconflict land administration. The succession of radical displacements of populations and serial refugee returns by different ethnic groups created special difficulties for restitution of land to returnees and in some areas led the government to adopt the expedience of "land sharing," requiring those with conflicting claims to the land to divide the contested land among their households. In the early stages of the refugee return, the government opted to resettle many returnees in villages rather than returning them to home sites on their homesteads. This created a new set of land issues, because the rights to the land utilized were often not ascertained, and land for cultivation was often not available in the vicinity.

These issues complicate a land situation that was problematic even before the war. Rwanda has a total population of 9.9 million, with an average population density of 479 persons per square kilometer, ranging from 640 persons per square kilometer in the northwest to 466 persons per square kilometer in the southeast (Sagashya and English 2010). A population growth rate of over 3 percent per year has resulted in all land being occupied and subject to increasing pressure, overuse, and fragmentation (Musahara and Huggins 2005), a situation often characterized as "Malthusian" (Andre and Platteau 1998). Land distribution is skewed, with 24 percent of households controlling roughly 70 percent of the country's arable land and over a third of rural households holding only about one-tenth of a hectare. Holdings are typically fragmented into several parcels. The country has a long history of intense competition over land and grievances over land dispossessions, often framed in terms of ethnic conflict between Hutu and Tutsi. (For a historical perspective on today's policy discussions, see Pottier 2006.) In these circumstances, the attainment of security of tenure was an urgent concern of the postwar government, which began with reform of the law on land and land administration.

Prior to the war, customary land tenure prevailed in most of the county. A 1976 Land Law recognized both customary and registered ownership rights. Registered private ownership was under a Torrens-style title registration system introduced during the colonial period, initially for Belgian settlers, but later utilized by Rwandese elites as well. Postindependence legislation limited property rights in registered land to long-term use rights. Many of the registered parcels were urban, but some large rural estates were registered under the system as well, and this increased pressure on land in the vicinity. Estimates of the amount of land in registered titles at independence are generally under 10 percent of land. Obtaining information on the operation of this system is difficult (Musahara and Huggins 2005).

In the immediate postwar period, the old Torrens-based system continued in force. In theory, it had been accessible to all Rwandese since before independence, but in practice its complexity and the high costs involved largely excluded all but the wealthiest from its use. Although the title registration model is preferred by most authorities on land administration, the version in force in Rwanda was antiquated, unduly complex and expensive, and quite unable to cope with the reality of the country in the late 20th century.

In 1997, some three years after the end of the civil war and 1994 genocide, the government started work on a new Land Law. This led to a contentious policy debate between those who favored a property-rights approach and those who favored a more top-down planning approach. The new law, which reflects an uneasy compromise between these approaches, was only finalized and enacted in July 2005. It seeks to address the insecurity involved in land sharing, resettlement, and consolidation of fragmented landholdings. The law provides that all land belongs to the Rwandese people, is managed by the state, and is made available to private users under leases of between 3 and 99 years, made by new local land commissions. These leaseholds may be transferred or mortgaged, but this requires the consent of spouses and children. Customary holdings are to be converted to these leaseholds held from the state; customary tenure and its institutions are abolished. Registration of land rights is mandatory, and the law authorizes systematic registration, to be provided for in detail in regulations. Transfers of leasehold rights do not affect third parties unless they are registered (Organic Law No. 08/2005 of 14/07/2005 Determining the Use and Management of Land in Rwanda).

Although the law in general terms guarantees proprietors the right to use and enjoy their land, it requires compliance with a master plan and contains quite specific requirements regarding conservation and productivity. Where private users have failed to exploit or have degraded the land they hold, they are to be given six months' notice, and then the government can intervene and give the land to another person to use, though the original leaseholder can apply for its return. In the case of land degradation or persistent failure to produce, the land may be forcibly confiscated by the government without resort to the courts. There is a major dichotomy in the law. On one hand, there are provisions intended to enhance security of tenure to create incentives and enable farmers' responses to markets. But on the other, there are provisions that reflect a strong antimarket inclination on the part of the government, seeking to enforce efficient land use and allowing local governments to compel consolidation of fragmented holdings (see Pottier 2006 for a critical discussion of the law).

MINITERE, the ministry responsible for land, now renamed the Ministry of Natural Resources (MINIRENA), launched an ambitious program to implement the law through a program of systematic ("mass") tenure regularization. The program is being carried out with technical assistance provided by the U.K.'s Department for International Development (DFID). A strategic roadmap was developed and presented at a 2007 workshop (MINITERE 2007a). The program proceeded in two phases: from 2005 to 2007, Phase I focused on development of a strategic road map, trial interventions, and phasing of reforms, while Phase II (full implementation) began in 2009.

There has been intensive work on subsidiary legislation to flesh out the Land Law, including rules for systematic land registration, and more than 20 such subsidiary enactments have been promulgated or are under consideration. The government has also established needed institutional structures within MINIRENA: a National Land Commission, and below that a National Land Centre, in which the Land Registry is located.

Surveys and field consultations to test the waters for systematic land registration were begun in 2006 in Musanze, Kirehe, Karongi, and Gasabo Districts.

One finding was that there was a thriving land market and that people were demanding a stronger role for the state and written proof of land rights. The report concluded that systematic "people-led" land registration could work in Rwanda. One of the more challenging tasks, the report noted, would be to provide clear rules for the translation of customary rights, which tend to be complex and multilayered, into simple leases. From the outset, it was clear that customary rights were to be replaced with rights from the state, and so the initiative was a major land tenure reform as well as a formalization program (MINITERE 2006).

The implementation process, referred to as "tenure regularization" (MINITERE 2007b), began with implementation trials in 2007 in selected cells (the most local administrative subdivision) in the same four districts covered in the survey. The trials involved systematic demarcation, adjudication, and registration of titles in a process designed to be participatory. Fees for holdings of less than five hectares were minimal and affordable even for poor families. Existing parcels were demarcated but not surveyed, and rights were adjudicated by a locally elected committee through a transparent and open process. Results were published locally. Disputed ownership and boundaries were identified separately and objections noted, with disputes referred to the *abunzi* (customary courts as reconstituted by the government), subject to the agreement of the disputants. For each parcel where there was an uncontested claim, a long-term lease was granted automatically, based upon the adjudication record, and the title registered. The pilot work covered 3,513 households and some 15,000 parcels. Based on the pilot work, procedures for clarifying and confirming rights in land were detailed in a Ministerial Order Determining the Modalities of Land Registration (Order No. 002/2008) (Sagashya and English 2010).

A recent World Bank evaluation of the impacts of the pilot registration found that only 2.5 years after completion of the pilot, a large majority of those involved viewed the process as fair and transparent (Ali et al. 2010). Land-attached investment (and maintenance of existing structures) was found to be significantly higher in the areas registered than in the control areas. The high frequency of land transfers suggested a need to urgently complement the field work with the establishment of the facilities needed to register transactions and inheritances. This was required to keep the register up-to-date and ensure sustainability of benefits. The report rejects the hypothesis that the transfers were distress sales or that they disproportionately involved female landholders, which had been raised as a concern by some observers. More effective promotion of legal literacy, especially in the urban areas, was urged. Some parcels could not be registered because of ongoing disputes. This involved a considerable proportion of parcels in urban areas, around 11 percent, but was less of a problem in rural areas.

The DFID is funding the rollout of this program and will contribute £20 million over 2009–14 to enable the now-established National Land Centre to register an estimated 8 million parcels of land and to establish the land administration machinery to make the program sustainable. As of 2010, the program had demarcated more than 2.2 million plots, progressing at a rate of around

250,000 plots per month. A total of 456 field teams (about 4,000 staff) are work-ing in all 30 districts of Rwanda. The field work is backed up by data entry staff in five sites across the country, a team of geographic information system experts, and a dedicated print room producing maps, printouts of aerial photographs for the field teams, and leases (DFID 2010; Sagashya and English 2010).

The obvious attraction of the land regularization program ("regularization" and "registration" are used interchangeably in this context) is that it promises to end the long period of uncertainty and insecurity of land rights ushered in by the war and genocide. Implementation has been relatively smooth, and initial evalu-ations of impacts are encouraging. Exactly how much tenure security the regis-tration will provide will become clear only in time. The government's land policy contains contradictory elements, and although this case study necessarily focuses on the land administration dimension of "the land question" in Rwanda, these should not be overlooked when it comes to developing an effective, postconflict response to land issues.

Indeed, quite apart from the underlying social and ethnic aspects of land occu-pation and use in Rwanda, new policy elements are actively provoking tensions in a landscape where reducing them should be the major objective. Although the regularization program seeks to reestablish security of tenure, there is also an active program of compulsory land consolidation. This was presaged in a 2007 Rwanda Agricultural Land Use Consolidation Strategy, leading to promulgation of a Decree on Agricultural Land Use Consolidation later that year. In February 2008, the Ministry of Agriculture and Animal Resources (MINAGRI) ordered consolidation of land use in certain areas, specifying that maize must be grown rather than sweet potatoes, with seeds provided free of charge.

Under this new decree, if fields are not prepared for maize by a specific date, the land is given to others to farm. Not only does this raise evident concerns about security of tenure and run contrary to the spirit of the tenure regulariza-tion, it also raises the specter of preconflict tensions over land. The decree applies only in the *marai* (critical marshlands). Many of those were converted from pasture (the traditional land use of Tutsi pastoralists) to farmland (for use by Hutu cultivators) in the conflict years. The decree is also applicable to areas where land has recently been formalized. Concerns have been expressed that this will undermine the objective of the regularization program, conveying to land-holders that their land is less than secure, whether or not it is registered. The case underscores that the government has, through the registration program, opted for regularizing the status quo, rather than reopening land "justice" issues coming out of the conflict. Only time will tell if this approach delivers on peace in the land sector (Bruce 2009).

Agricultural land use consolidation is a significant factor threatening efforts to reestablish land tenure security, but it is not the only factor. Large numbers of refugees remain outside the country, principally in the Democratic Republic of Congo, and it remains unclear how they will be accommodated if and when they return. As of December 2013, United Nations High Commissioner for Refugees (UNHCR) statistics show 141,190 Rwandese refugees in the Democratic

Republic of Congo. Much smaller numbers exist in Burundi, Tanzania, and Uganda (UNHCR 2011). How will their land claims be handled when they return? Further "land sharing" would clash with the government's efforts to institute tenure security, and again raise questions about the value of a registered title. Land sharing may in fact still be taking place on a small scale in some localities.

To sum up, after the end of the conflict the government of Rwanda moved relatively rapidly to develop a major land initiative intended to institute security of tenure. The core of the initiative is conversion of customary rights to leaseholds from the state and systematic registration of those smallholdings. This program has been carried out remarkably quickly and competently, in part because of strong and timely bilateral assistance.

On the other hand, the program was embarked upon without sufficient public consultation and, perhaps most critically, without a consensus within government and civil society over underlying policy issues, in particular the balance to be struck between tenure security, the role of local structures, and government land management interventions such as land consolidation. That balance is still being negotiated, although not through the systematic and open policy debate in Kigali one might wish to see, but rather throughout the country via decisions made by officials acting at the local level. Anecdotal evidence suggests that rather than interacting creatively with local leadership, officials may sometimes be applying their own interpretations of policy and overriding local concerns.

More broadly, the nationwide land registration approach taken by Rwanda to secure tenure postconflict was greatly facilitated by substantial foreign assistance and the country's relatively small size. More highly participatory models are available with lower cost implications, such as the one recently carried out in Ethiopia (see chapter 3). In a situation of continuing ethnic tensions in which customary land tenure systems were implicated, reliance on and upgrading of those systems to provide tenure security, an option often favored, was problematic. Another cost-effective approach, the delimitation and certification of community (rather than household) rights, as pursued in Mozambique, would have been difficult in a context in which "communities" were rent by ethnic division and the rebuilding of social consensus at a community level was a major national challenge. The approach taken makes sense in Rwandese circumstances, but whether the system will prove sustainable depends heavily upon landholders taking the initiative to register their inheritances and transactions; elsewhere they have often failed to do so (see chapter 3).

## Liberia's Postconflict Land Administration

In the wake of a decade of civil war and abuse of authority, Liberia's land administration situation was dire. Liberia has a strong legal tradition of private land ownership, originating in the system of grants and later sales of freeholds to liberated slaves and black freemen returning from America beginning in the 1820s. This system is solidly grounded in Liberia's constitution, statute, and common law. A deed registry system originating in the 1850s provided a process of validation and public recording of new deeds. Later, some local notables from indigenous groups were also able to obtain titles, or "aboriginal deeds," as they were called.

As in many African countries, government sales of land considered "public" but in fact held by indigenous peoples under customary right caused deep resentment. Early on, settlers bought land along the coast from the native inhabitants, but later land in the interior was considered public land by right of conquest. The public land sale system is the origin of virtually all private ownership titles in the interior of the country and is the mechanism by which settlers and their descendants (Americo-Liberians) dispossessed indigenous populations. Resentment generated over time by this process contributed directly to the 1980 military overthrow of the elected government, dominated by the descendants of settlers, and started Liberia down the track to civil war. It is clear that any land administration solution must not only address technical formalization concerns but must also seek to resolve historically rooted land grievances if peace is to survive and prosper.

Indeed, Liberia faces a wide range of land management challenges in its postconflict period. First, the government's capability to handle land policy and administration is in a badly degraded state and authority over land within the government is badly fragmented. Second, Liberia's preconflict legal framework is antiquated and inadequate to address the postconflict challenges. Third, several major land issues hold the potential to revive tensions, from both before and after the conflict.

The Ministry of Lands, Mines and Energy (MLME) is entrusted with land administration today and carries out this task through its Department of Lands, Surveys and Cartography (DLSC). Land administration is carried out using preconflict statutes, many of which are antiquated. The DLSC, having been ousted from its former office during the conflict, occupies a run-down rented office some distance from the main ministry office. Although programs under the Departments of Mining and Energy, the two other competencies of the MLME, received attention because they offered revenue potentials for the cash-strapped government, rebuilding land administration does not seem to have been a priority.

Primary responsibility for land administration lies in MLME, but the ministry has no real coordination mandate for the land sector. Sectoral ministries such as Agriculture make agricultural concessions and declare nature reserves with little coordination with those with technical responsibility for land administration. The Deed Registry is located outside MLME, in the Center for National Documentation, Records and Archives (CNDRA). Anomalously, the older land registers are held in the Foreign Ministry. The CNDRA lost its facility during the war but was able to move back into one floor in 2009 and had taken over the whole building by 2013. With modest assistance from the World Bank and other donors, it is seeking to reequip and renovate its facilities.

Each county has a County Land Commissioner, a presidential appointee who reports to the Minister of Interior and through him to the President. There is also the County Surveyor, who reports to the MLME's DLSC; the County Probate Court, which authenticates deeds; and the County Deed Registry, reporting to the CNDRA. This machinery handles the public land sale program at the county level. Public land sales, the origin of most titles in the interior of Liberia, are handled by the country Land Commissioner in direct coordination with the Office of the Presidency. The Commissioner passes completed sale documents to the Probate Court, which authenticates the sale, confirming the identity of the parties and ensuring that the proper steps have been taken. Once approved by the Probate Court, the land sale documents are sent to the Deed Registry for registration. Sales and inheritances of land are similarly processed through the Probate Court prior to being sent to the Deeds Registry for recording.

Many deed records were looted during the war or exposed to the elements. They are in a state of serious disrepair, many crumbling, and still have not all been brought under control of the legally responsible agency, CNDRA. The Deed Registry system has long been criticized as outmoded and not suitable for the modern needs of the land sector. Deed registration provides weak tenure security only made tolerable by landholders purchasing title insurance policies; such insurance is not and has never been available in Liberia (Bentsi-Enchill and Zarr 1966). The probate courts, critical to the operation of the system, ceased to operate during the conflict and today are only semifunctional (Paczynska 2010).

Concerns about the adequacy of the Deed Registry and the effectiveness and probity of its administration existed even before the civil war, and the land sector institutions can only be described as seriously degraded by years of conflict. There is a striking competence gap between the few remaining older staff members at the top, who received solid technical training before 1980, and the many junior staff, most of whom lack technical skills. Management systems are weak. Because of the loss of many original documents and some registers, fraud and other malpractice have flourished in the postwar period, and there are indications that some registry employees have been involved in fraud and tampering with land records. The system is functioning, but its trustworthiness is highly questionable.

The ongoing program most affected by these inadequacies is the public land sale program, controversial both for the role it has played in shifting land ownership to the Americo-Liberian community and for the corruption that has long characterized it. Serious underlying causes of tensions over land contributed directly to the build-up toward the civil war. The manner in which they are dealt with in postconflict Liberia will have critical consequences in the longer term. In recognition of the sensitivity of this issue, the President in February 2010 placed a three-month moratorium on public land sales, which was later extended and is still in force as of early January 2014. At her request, the Land Commission established a screening committee to vet all public land sale deeds awaiting her signature. In March 2011 the Land Commission approved Interim Guidelines and Procedures for the Sale of Public Land. The guidelines address some major problems and sales may resume soon, but the resolution of other problems awaits new legislation on public land management. Pending legislation, they leave open the question of whether a public land sale program can play a useful role in public land management in Liberia today.

No reliable statistics are available on the amount of land within the Deed Registry system, or the portion of land within Liberia that has been formalized. It is commonly assumed that most of the land for which public land sale deeds have issued has been brought within the system. This would include most of the land in a belt 30–40 miles wide along the coast, corresponding to the early areas of colonial settlement, and more limited areas of land along major roads and in town centers in the interior. The extent to which subsequent sales and successions to that land have been registered is unclear. The poor quality of the original parcel identification in deeds (many using "metes and bounds," which is a system that uses physical features of the local geography to give directions and distances to describe the boundaries of the parcel) makes locating even registered parcels difficult.

Liberia also has a second land registration system, at least on paper. In 1974 a Land Registration Law based on the Torrens "title registration" model was enacted (Chapter 8, Liberian Code of Laws Revised).[1] It was to be implemented through the survey, adjudication, and registration of titles in areas to which it was declared to apply, and it was anticipated that it would gradually expand to replace the Deed Registry system. The new system provided a comprehensive parcel map in which parcel registers reflected the land rights in the parcels, which once registered were difficult to challenge, providing strong tenure security. The organizational structure for implementation for the new law draws upon the existing machinery used for Deed Registration. There is still a special role for the probate court, and the Registrar of Deeds is also the Registrar of Lands. The Registrar of Lands is located in the National Archives, as is the Registrar of Deeds.

Systematic registration is set in motion when the Minister of Lands, Mines and Energy declares through the local probate court that titles in a specified area will be adjudicated and registered. Holdings are demarcated and the claims recorded. A referee hears and decides disputes, and in deciding upon claims is to base decisions upon good documentary title, or failing that, open, peaceful, and interrupted possession for 20 years or more. If there is a possessor who is unable to provide sufficient proof to be registered as an owner, he can be tentatively recorded as owner subject to substantiation within six months. If no private rights are established, the land should be recorded as public land. A party unhappy with the decision of the referee may appeal to the Supreme Court.

It should be noted that the two systems share a fundamental shortcoming. Neither system makes adequate provision for registration of customary rights, under which most rural land in Liberia is held. Recognition of these rights is the single most fundamental policy issue facing Liberia, and one that must be clearly addressed before they can be brought effectively within any system of titling and registration. Research is currently under way at several sites in

Liberia to assess customary land tenure, funded by the Millennium Challenge Corporation (MCC) and implemented by the Land Commission and Tetra Tech ARD.

The systematic registration approach was piloted in areas of serious contention over land in Monrovia in the late 1970s and early 1980s. This was an area in which private land rights under deed had already been established. The United Nations Development Programme (UNDP) and other donors supported the effort, with technical expertise provided by the U.K.'s Directorate of Overseas Surveys. But the 1980 military coup caused a loss of focus on implementation, and soon governance problems arose. There was political intervention in adjudications, and land was put forward for registration in the name of powerful individuals although those individuals lacked any documentation to support their claims. Donors soon withdrew. The result is that the machinery needed to update the new systematic registrations as transactions and inheritance took place was never established, and even today transfers of the land in the pilot areas are recorded in the Deed Registry.

From the reestablishment of peace in 2003 until 2007, little was done to resuscitate the land administration system, and significant assistance did not arrive until 2008–09. The United Nations Mission in Liberia did call for deposit of deeds and other land documentation for preservation, but no significant international support for rebuilding the land administration institutions was received during the immediate postwar period. Because exports of forest products from Liberia were embargoed in the immediate postconflict period, the government focused heavily on a new Forestry Law (and a later Community Forestry Law). This led to what was often a discussion of land rights, including rights to forested land under custom, but one that suffered from being focused too exclusively on a single land use (Wily 2007).

During 2003–09, much of the attention of the international community was focused on land dispute resolution. In some counties with endemic land disputes, especially Bong and Nimba Counties, these were addressed quite effectively by nongovernmental organizations (NGOs; notably the Norwegian Refugee Council) using alternative dispute resolution approaches. Ad hoc land commissions were employed less successfully by the government to address high-tension areas. These efforts were aimed at preventing such disputes from sparking new violence. Ultimately, however, land dispute resolution addresses the symptoms rather than the causes of land disputes, and the solution to many of the problems facing Liberian landholders lies in the removal of legal uncertainty and insecurity through reform and the development of a system of property rights and land administration that also fully addresses the key issue of customarily held and managed land.

The government is aware of these needs, as indicated by MLME documents from 2006 (Government of Liberia 2006a, 2006b).[2] Those documents endorse the conversion from deeds registration to title registration under the 1974 law but give no sense of any appreciation of the magnitude of that task. Such conversions, based on experience in other countries, are the work of a generation.

If such an enterprise were undertaken, the Deed Registration system during an interim period would need to remain in operation in those parts of the country to which the new system has not yet been extended through systematic survey and adjudication. The two systems would need to be operated in parallel, for all practical purposes.

The policy and legal issues posed are clearly challenging and politically sensitive. In 2007–08, Liberia's Governance Commission, which had been considering land issues, reached the conclusion that a separate Land Commission, independent of existing government structures, was needed. An Interim Working Group on Land with broad official stakeholder representation developed plans for the Land Commission and prepared a draft law to create it. The new Land Commission was created by an act of the legislature in mid-2009. Appointed by the President, it became operational around the middle of 2010, with a planned five-year lifetime, extendable for two additional years if needed.

The mandate of the commission is to propose policy and law reforms and to coordinate all government activities in the land sector. Its role is facilitation rather than direct involvement in implementation. This, together with the commission's advocacy of donor support for existing land sector institutions, has ensured the support of the line ministries for the commission and avoided turf battles with them. The MLME has been an active and supportive participant in discussions leading up to the creation of the commission and in the deliberations of its working groups. This reflects the conviction of MLME officials that only a broad national effort can bring about the needed changes and lead to stronger institutional arrangements for land administration.

The decision to create the Land Commission was an important signal to the donor community of the need to address these issues. UNDP, UN-HABITAT, and the World Bank provided early assistance to the Governance Commission in the lead-up to creation of the Land Commission, and UN-HABITAT provided critical and flexible early assistance to the Land Commission. The World Bank and the MCC (under its Liberia Threshold Program) provided funding to the Commission, the DLSC, and the Deed Registry. More recently, the Swedish International Development Cooperation Agency became an important donor via support to UN-HABITAT's assistance to the Commission, which has focused on alternative land dispute resolution.

Very substantial resources have now been placed behind the work of the Commission and other land sector agencies. A Donor Coordination Committee on Land was formed in 2009 and is working closely with the Land Commission and other land sector agencies. A government budget covers basic institutional costs, such as the salaries of the commissioners. Donor funding is supporting digitization and conservation of land records and studies of (1) public land sale procedures and problems, (2) factors explaining the failure of the systematic land registration pilot two decades ago, (3) reforms needed for the Deed Registry system, (4) customary land law and its interface with  formal systems, and (5) needs and strategies for development of a land policy and land law reform. Equipment and training are being provided to both the DLSC and the Deed Registry. Efforts are under way to coordinate the many local and international NGOs carrying out alternative land dispute resolution.

These are positive steps, although taken later than might have been hoped. They signal a clear intention on the part of the government to seriously address land issues, including underlying sociological factors that are long-standing causes of the tensions over land that led to civil war in the first place. It remains to be seen how long it will take for the Commission to provide the clear policy directions and legal framework needed to resuscitate land administration in Liberia. In 2011 the Commission approved a Strategy for Reform of Liberia's Civil Law Concerning Land based on a World Bank–funded study by the commission (Bruce and Kanneh 2011), but the 2012 presidential election stalled the work of the Commission for nearly a year.

Approaching these issues through an independent commission has much to recommend it, but such commissions also have potential downsides, including a temptation to perpetuate what is intended as a short-term initiative. The Commission's focus on its mandate has been diluted by pressures from the Office of the Presidency to involve itself directly in land dispute resolution, and by the need to contend with the awkward results of extensive and controversial grants of large-scale forest and agricultural concessions to foreign investors.

The concession issue raises questions about how effectively the Commission is able to perform its broad coordination mandate. It was not able to stem the concession granting by line ministries and other sectoral agencies and finds itself in damage-control mode instead. It has recommended a moratorium on new concessions to the President, to give time to assess and deal with the issues around concessions already granted and to develop sounder policy and procedures in this area; the President has so far not acted upon that recommendation.

In the face of these fundamental policy issues, rebuilding capacity in the MLME has lagged. This is in part due to weak leadership in that institution, but other factors will challenge those developing policy and strategy for future land administration. Many Liberians perceive land survey and registration as having played a negative role in a painful history of land grabbing from local landholders through public land sales and concessions. This will complicate the policy discussion around the reform and rebuilding of the country's land administration system. The dominant role of private ownership in the areas long under this form of tenure (the coastal belt and limited areas in the interior) does not seem to be challenged, but it is quite possible that different land tenure policies and land administration tools will be recommended by the Commission for the land still effectively under local custom in the interior of the country. Options such as the Ethiopian low-cost and participatory household land certification and the group land certification in Mozambique are under consideration.

## Rebuilding: Lessons Learned

The experiences of Rwanda and Liberia suggest some lessons for postconflict countries dealing with land administration issues:

- Governments should be encouraged to confront and deal with land issues as early as possible in a postconflict situation, as an integral part of any peace-building strategy; the donor community must also come in with solid support as early as possible and as part of its own peace-building program for countries in this situation.

- Multilateral agencies such as UNHCR that engage early in the postconflict period must support the government to:
  - Develop strategies to address not only the short-term issues associated with restitution but also, with support from development agencies, the longer-term underlying social and political causes of land tensions, and
  - Develop sound policies for land administration and management.

- Simply rehabilitating national land administration institutions and the courts that deal with land disputes is a necessary but not sufficient condition for ensuring long-term security and preventing land from becoming a conflict trigger again in the future. Underlying sources of tension must be addressed.

- Both international and local NGOs are used by relief agencies and donors in short-term roles they might not normally take on pending the reestablishment of government capacity, such as land dispute resolution. This is a valid strategy as long as parallel work begins very shortly thereafter to rebuild government capacity.

- Various options are available for addressing the needs of postconflict governments:
  - Early consultancies by national and international consultants or NGOs with expertise in the land field can be valuable in initially assessing needs;
  - Recourse by UNHCR and other humanitarian agencies to multilateral agencies with competence in the land area, such as the Food and Agriculture Organization's (FAO's) Land Tenure Service, the World Bank, or UN-HABITAT, can help provide needed expertise and funding;
  - Earlier engagement by bilateral donors with substantial experience in the land field, such as DFID, the United States Agency for International Development (USAID), and GTZ, can also provide expertise and funding.

- Donors need to reconsider the criteria under which "peace-building" funds are available for early commitment in postconflict countries. These are typically too narrowly focused on short-term needs and immediate results. The hunger for short-term results is understandable, but can delay national institutions from resuming their proper roles.

- That said, capacity building and achievement of results are not incompatible. In Rwanda implementation of the program of systematic land registration, which has engaged thousands of staff, is creating new capacity. Learning-by-doing even very modest tasks is possible but may require reliance on simple technologies in early stages. Relief agencies should involve government staff of the ministry responsible for land matters in any programs having to do with land.

- In countries that have suffered prolonged conflict, the need for retraining should not be underestimated. The institutions that deal with land may need skill rebuilding at all levels, not just for technical skills but also for very basic training of existing staff in financial and personnel management.

- To enrich and open up discussions of policy to a broader national audience, it may be useful for donors and other actors to support the creation or evolution of one or more local "land NGOs," with particular competence in this area. Where possible, these should be membership organizations.

- A balance needs to be struck between a prompt response to the need for action and spending time reaching a political and social consensus on policy prior to designing and implementing reforms to land management and land administration systems. The right balance will differ from country to country, and will depend in part on the political stability of the government. Donors may usefully act as a counterbalance, urging action or caution, as appropriate. In Rwanda, experts often found themselves encouraging the government to go slower, to consult and test before committing to major lines of action. In Liberia a national Land Commission was created to facilitate a considered approach, but there is a risk it will fail to deliver solutions fast enough.

- The postconflict period is challenging in many respects, but it is also a period of opportunity. There is often an appreciation on the part of policy makers that fundamental changes are needed and a fear of return to conflict that can incentivize reforms. This period is also a time when vested interests may be disorganized and less effective. It may be possible to address deep and long held grievances that create conflicts. This window of opportunity for reform must be taken advantage of quickly, before it closes.

- Where fundamental reforms are needed, it will usually be helpful to create mechanisms and institutions that reach beyond land sector agencies. Those agencies often have vested interests, which make them unlikely proponents of reforms. Such new institutions or mechanisms will likely be more effective in pursuing the policy and legal reform agenda if not also tasked with dispute resolution and reform implementation. This will avoid turf battles with line ministries. It is equally important, however, that the land sector agency staff be involved in the policy discussion and reform design, both for their substantive contributions and to build in them a sense of ownership of the reform that will be critical to effective implementation.

## Notes

1. For a fuller description of the law, see World Bank (2008), annex E.
2. A 150-Day Plan of Action (March 1, 2006) identifies various key needs in the land sector, citing the lack of a national land policy, a national institutional framework for land administration that is "improperly designed, uncoordinated and ineffective," confusion as to responsibility for management of public lands, and a dismal lack of trained staff, facilities, and equipment. A "Memorandum of Understanding for the Conceptual Understanding of the Challenges to Land Title and Registration and Corresponding Resolutions to Said Challenges" (October 21, 2006) identifies problems as "1) lack of coordination between ministries, 2) lack of transparency, 3) lack of information, 4) lack of coordinated adjudication system, 5) lack of complete clear chain of title and land records." It calls for measures to "ensure the effectiveness of the deed system while fast tracking the conversion to a title registration system."

## References

Ali, D. A., K. Deininger, M. Goldstein, and M. Stickler. 2010. "Case Study: Pilot Land Tenure Registration in Rwanda: Evidence of Initial Impacts." World Bank, Washington, DC.

Andre, C., and J. P. Platteau. 1998. "Land Relations under Unbearable Stress: Rwanda Caught in the Malthusian Trap." *Journal of Economic Behavior and Organization* 34 (1): 1–47.

Bentsi-Enchill, K., and G. H. Zarr. 1966. "The Assurance of Land Titles and Transactions in Liberia." *Liberian Law Journal* 2: 94–121.

Bruce, J. W. 2009. "Reform of the Policy and Legal Framework." Paper presented at UN-HABITAT Land and Conflict Workshop in Nairobi as input into Land and Conflict Guidelines "Toolkit and Guidance for Preventing and Managing Land and Natural Resources Conflict: Land and Conflict." UN-HABITAT (2012), September 2009. http://www.un.org/en/events/environmentconflictday/pdf/GN_Land_Consultation.pdf.

Bruce, J. W., and B. Kanneh. 2011. *Reform of Liberia's Civil Law Concerning Land; A Proposed Strategy*. Report to the Land Commission, Monrovia.

DFID (Department for International Development). 2010. "UK Registers Land in Kigali." DFID, London.

Government of Liberia, Ministry of Land, Mines and Energy (MLME). 2006a. "One Hundred and Fifty (150) Day Action Plan: Enhancing Government's Effectiveness in Managing the Land, Mineral and Energy Sectors." March 1, MLME, Monrovia.

———. 2006b. "Memorandum of Understanding for the Conceptual Understanding of the Challenges to Land Title and Registration and Corresponding Resolutions to Said Challenges." October 21, MLME, Monrovia.

Leckie, S., and C. Huggins. 2011. *Conflict and Housing, Land and Property Rights. A Handbook on Issues, Frameworks and Solutions.* Cambridge, U.K.: Cambridge University Press.

MINITERE. 2006. "Minitere Field Consultations: March–October 2006." MINITERE, Kigali.

———. 2007a. "The Road Map to Land Reform, A Simple Model." MINITERE, Kigali.

———. 2007b. "Summary of Proposed Trials Work 2007: From Strategy to 10 Year Plan." MINITERE, Kigali.

Musahara, H., and C. Huggins. 2005. "Land Reform, Land Scarcity, and Post-Conflict Reconstruction: A Case Study of Rwanda." In *From the Ground Up: Land Rights, Conflict and Peace in Sub-Saharan Africa*, edited by C. Huggins and J. Clover, 269–346. Pretoria: Institute of Security Studies.

Paczynska, A. 2010. *Liberia Interagency Conflict Assessment Framework Report.* State Department, Washington, DC.

Pottier, J. 2006. "Land Reform for Peace? Rwanda's 2005 Land Law in Context." *Journal of Agrarian Change* 6 (4): 509–37.

Sagashya, D., and C. English. 2010. "Designing and Establishing a Land Administration System for Rwanda: Technical and Economic Analysis." Joint Discussion Paper of World Bank, GLTN, FIG, and FAO, in *Innovations in Land Rights Recognition, Administration and Governance*, edited by K. Deininger, C. Augustinus, S. Enemark, and P. Munro-Faure, 43–59. Washington, DC: World Bank.

Tanner, C. 2002. "Law-making in an African Context: The 1997 Mozambique Land Law." FAO Legal Papers Online No. 26, FAO, Rome.

UNHCR. 2011. "Rwanda Refugee Status Report." http://www.unhcr.org/pages/49e45c576 .html.

Wily, L. A. 2007. *So Who Owns the Forest: An Investigation into Forest Ownership and Customary Land Rights in Liberia.* Sustainable Development Initiative and FERN, Monrovia and Brussels.

World Bank. 2008. *Insecurity of Land Tenure, Land Law and Land Registration in Liberia.* AFR Report 46134-LR, Washington, DC.

# CHAPTER 5

# Developing Land Information Systems in Sub-Saharan Africa: Experiences and Lessons from Uganda and Ghana

Mykhailo Cheremshynskyi and Frank F. K. Byamugisha

## Introduction

Although only about 10 percent of Africa's rural land is registered, leaving 90 percent of the land informally administered, formal land administration still plays an important role in securing land tenure. Given that registered land is often the more productive part of the total stock of land, effective land administration contributes to both shared and sustained economic growth and to reducing land disputes that, if unchecked, could escalate into major conflicts. However, in most African countries, governments face difficulties in establishing the institutional and legal framework necessary for "good land administration" and often lack accurate and reliable land information (World Bank Institute 2006).

The malfunctions of land administration systems that impede economic development in many African countries have been discussed and analyzed in many studies, publications, and project reports (Deininger and Feder 2009). Many of the traditional cadastral and land registration systems, with their complex institutional structures inherited from the colonial past, are outdated and unable to satisfy a growing demand for services. This partly explains why it takes twice as long (65 days) and costs twice as much (9.4 percent of property value) to transfer land in Sub-Saharan Africa (SSA) than in Organisation for Economic Co-operation and Development (OECD) countries (31 days; 4.4 percent) (World Bank 2012).

An information system that can provide affordable, timely, and accurate information about land resources and their quantity, quality, ownership, and use is a cornerstone of any land administration and land management system. Establishment of such a system is not just a technical, technological, or organizational matter, but rather a complex task that touches on many social, economic, and political aspects. Successful establishment requires a holistic vision of the system, systematic and innovative approaches to its implementation, an update of the legal framework, changes in the institutional structure of land administration, and a reengineering of existing procedures. But the opportunity to establish a Land Information System (LIS) that replaces traditional cadastral and land registration infrastructure and increases the availability and quality of land administration services for businesses, banks, and the population at large has never been greater because of the development of new digital technologies during the last two decades: the availability of information and communication technologies (ICT), high-resolution satellite and aerial imagery, and the Global Positioning System (GPS), and the increasing affordability of these services.

In many countries in SSA, the performance of land administration is adversely affected by numerous issues, including inefficient procedures of land transactions, fragmentation of land administration systems, and fraudulent practices that are a cause of land conflicts and social instability (Byamugisha 2013). These issues are a manifestation of other problems commonly found in these countries, including a multiplicity of land tenure regimes and an absence of real mechanisms to manage them effectively and efficiently, a continual degradation of cadastral and registration records, poor service delivery from existing land administration institutions, lack of reliable and up-to-date information on land resources, and insufficient financial resources to support the maintenance of cadastral and registration systems. The two countries selected for this case study—Ghana and Uganda—have not been spared these issues.

This case study provides a review of the efforts and experience of Ghana and Uganda in developing and implementing computerized LISs. The study is based on an analysis of available publications, reports, and LIS project design documents in these countries as well as on the experience of the lead author in the design and/or implementation of these initiatives. These two countries were selected because they have been implementing LIS projects and have taken different approaches to their LIS design and implementation.

## The Basic Concept of LIS and the Relevance of New Technology

According to the UN Economic Commission for Europe (1996, 197), land administration is referred to as "the processes of determining, recording and disseminating information about the ownership, value and use of land, when implementing land management policies." A land administration system is thus the cornerstone of a secure land tenure system, which should guarantee access to the land, ensure equity in the distribution of land resources, eliminate gender discrimination in ownership, and preserve and conserve resources for future generations. Land administration practices and the structures of systems differ widely across countries throughout the world, reflecting historical, juridical, and cultural differences.

For a land administration system to meet its objectives, it must have up-to-date and reliable spatial data and other information about land. It should be able to provide answers to a few basic questions about land held, such as "what" (i.e., a description of the size of the land parcel, the land value, and its use), "where" the land parcel is located, and "how" the tenure is held. Such information was traditionally provided by cadastral systems, which in many countries were institutionally organized in the form of cadastral and land (title or deed) registers. A modern LIS can contribute greatly to the effectiveness and efficiency in answering those questions depending on how well the data are organized, stored, and accessed. In a broad sense, an LIS can refer to any data on either physical terrain features (e.g., topography, soil composition, geology, hydrology, vegetation density and species, climate), human aspects (e.g., population, land use, animal density, urban development, land productivity, erosion risks), or legal factors (e.g., use rights, ownership rights, land rights). However, building and maintaining an LIS that encompasses such a wide definition is a huge challenge, institutionally, methodologically, organizationally, and financially.

For land administration purposes, the definition of an LIS can be scaled down to satisfy the most important needs of the land administration process with essential information about land parcels and property in general. This includes information about parcels and property boundaries, their size, location, and other parcel-related features (geographic information), and tenure rights and interests (land records and documents). Such an LIS would also include a geometric (spatial) description of land parcels linked to other records (textual, attributive information) describing the nature of the interests and the ownership or control of those interests, as well as digital copies of relevant legal documents (titles and registrable instruments).

An innovative approach to the establishment of LIS-based opportunities provided by ICT in combination with best local practices to enhance its sustainability and affordability can help ensure the provision of land information to meet the needs of all groups of society. But without a holistic vision of the system and a strategy for its implementation, and without institutional changes and improvements, such an LIS cannot meet all the requirements mentioned above. As indicated by Falloux (1989), in many African countries, attempts to build country capacities in land are often supply driven, closely tied to the commercial or scientific interests of technology suppliers; changing this situation requires a demand-driven approach, based on understanding users' needs and their constraints.

## Experience in Developing an LIS

### Motivation for LIS Development in Ghana

In Ghana the main problems in land administration include (1) a multiplicity of land tenure regimes, (2) a small statutory land administration system running in parallel with a large informal land administration system managed by traditional authorities, (3) a deeds registration system running in parallel with a title registration system, and (4) outdated and poorly maintained manual land records (World Bank 2003). To address the issues in the land registration and administration systems, the government of Ghana prioritized the reform and modernization of land administration in its 15–25-year long-term land administration program, starting in 2003. Ghana's series of Land Administration Projects (LAPs) have been the main source of funding for the design and implementation of its LIS. LAP I was implemented from 2003 to 2010 (World Bank 2003), and LAP II began in 2011 and is due for completion in 2016 (World Bank 2011). Both LAP I and LAP II contained funding for improving land registration and administration systems, including the design and implementation of a computerized LIS. These were carried out as part of the activities of Component 3 of LAP I, which included also systematic land titling, registration, valuation, and development of the LIS. According to the terms of reference, the design of the LIS was planned to include three stages: (1) LIS design and development of six subsystems, (2) integration of the subsystems into one system, and (3) data conversion and upload to the system (Government of Ghana 2007).

The first stage was carried out in 2007 and 2008 and concentrated on addressing the immediate needs of the systematic land titling campaign in Accra and on LIS design. Stages 2 and 3 were planned to be tendered and initiated after the completion of the first stage or in parallel, depending on the results of the design (Government of Ghana 2007). The LIS design stage produced LIS Requirement, Design and Implementation Strategy Reports as well as various general recommendations regarding system development. Based on the government's request, the design stage also recommended the use of free/libre open source software (FLOSS) for LIS development (Johnson 2008).

In August 2009, a new study was carried out "to perform an initial assessment and prepare a detailed plan for the implementation of Open Source Cadastral and Registry (OSCAR) tools in Ghana" (Hall, Quaye, and Mensah 2009, 99). This study can be considered a continuation of efforts to determine the solution for Ghana's LIS design and implementation. The study provided a comprehensive report with a situation analysis, a baseline assessment, the requirements for system design, and recommendations on system specifications, an implementation plan, and terms of reference for a consultant to support implementation of OSCAR.

The implementation of OSCAR was to be done in phases over three years with support from the Food and Agricultural Organization (FAO). In general, phase one covers assessment, design, and coding of the common core code; phase two covers assessment, design, and customization in Ghana; and phase three covers deployment, testing, and training (Hall, Quaye, and Mensah 2009). The core software development and programming in phase one was planned to be carried out in Rome, and the customization was to be done in Ghana in phase two. Phase one was completed, but phase two was not completed, partly because of FAO running out of the required funds to support the project. And, of course, phase three could not start because phase two was not completed. Within the LAP but independent of the LIS, a Land Use Planning and Management Information System (LUPMIS) was designed and implemented. LUPMIS included the production of new orthophoto maps integrated with existing spatial data to support land use planning at the national, regional, district, and local levels.

In addition to the LAP, other projects related to the establishment of the LIS were implemented, such as the Urban Management Land Information System (UMLIS). The UMLIS pilot project, financed by the government of Ghana and the Swedish International Development Cooperation Agency (SIDA), was carried out in 2006–09 and aimed to support the establishment of the LIS in urban areas. The pilot project covered a relatively small pilot area, and the LIS database management system was developed based on a proprietary software environment (Microsoft SQL Server). The project was considered to support the LAP in prototyping some solutions, such as a database for land rent management based on property valuation that can be integrated with the structures of the LIS proposed in the LAP.

### Observations and Conclusions from Ghana's LIS Experience

Ghana's long-term land administration program, implemented through a series of LAPs, provides an appropriate funding framework to support development of an LIS. However, the LIS itself is a comprehensive, multifunctional information system, and the complexity of its development and implementation should not be underestimated. Development and implementation of such a system requires preparation of a structured program of activities whose implementation requires close coordination. This was not done in Ghana.

Although Ghana's LIS had all the building blocks in place or planned out, its development was done in a piecemeal fashion, without an adequate framework, blueprint, or road map to tie the pieces together or to guide their mutual development. For example, the development and installation of the initial LIS subsystems by COWI Consulting Engineers and Planners AS (COWI), the reengineering of business processes, the conversion of manual land records through so-called Intelligence Scanning, and the development of generic software in Rome and its subsequent attempts to customize it in Ghana were all undertaken independently and without careful sequencing. The various building blocks seem to have been initiated to address immediate problems and achieve quick wins, with integration considered only at the end. Ghana's potential quick wins included the use of scanned data, separate systems such as UMLIS and LUPMIS, and LIS subsystems for registration, valuation, survey, and mapping, and vested and public lands management. With the exception of UMLIS and LUPMIS, none of the potential quick wins have materialized so far. And integration of these pieces has not taken place either as of April 2014. An important challenge to future integration is coordination in systems development and a risk that some systems and subsystems might not communicate easily if at all. Global experience indicates that additional effort and resources will be required to achieve this given that appropriate detailed design and other measures were not taken upfront. The use of FLOSS and the Solutions for Open Land Administration software, if successfully undertaken, will reduce the dependency on licensed software, but will require significant effort in detailed design of LIS customization and system architecture, integration with other components required for land registration and cadastral procedures, and reengineering of business processes.

## Uganda's Experience in Developing LIS

### Motivation for LIS Development in Uganda

Uganda's main problems in land administration were related to the continuous degradation of its cadastral and registration records. These include "back door" corruptive practices, cumbersome and long procedures of land acquisition and title registration, fraudulent title certificates, and fraud in the administration of land rights. In addition, other factors that make improvement of the land administration systems complex include a multiplicity of registers (*mailo*, freehold, leasehold, and customary certificate records), outdated legislation in the area of title registration, and chronic understaffing and underfunding of land registration offices (World Bank 2004).

To address these problems, the government of Uganda undertook a comprehensive review of its land registration and administration systems early in the 1990s, which generated proposals for the rehabilitation of the systems (Greenwood 1990; Larsson 1990). Further studies undertaken between 1996 and 1998 found further deterioration in the registration and cadastral records and increasing backlogs of unsolved land cases; they stressed an urgent need to rehabilitate existing land records and to develop a computerized LIS. In response to these findings and study recommendations, the government of Uganda prioritized the modernization of land registration and administration in its 10-year Land Sector Strategic Plan (LSSP; 2001–11) (Government of Uganda 2004). As part of the LSSP implementation, various background studies were carried out in 2001–06, concentrating on different aspects of land administration as well as the feasibility of designing and implementing a computerized LIS. In 2007–08 the architecture design of the LIS framework was carried out under the Land Component of the Second Private Sector Competitiveness Project (PSCP II), financed by the World Bank (2004). The LIS architecture design produced a comprehensive baseline assessment of the situation in the land administration sector, a preliminary design for the LIS, and terms of reference for the "Design, Supply, Installation, and Implementation of the LIS and Securing of Land Records," which was completed in February 2013.

The overall objective of the so-called LIS Project was to improve efficiency and transparency in land registration and administration systems. The project had many stakeholders, but the main client was Uganda's Ministry of Lands, Housing and Urban Development (MLHUD). The technical specifications for the LIS and the strategy for implementation were based on the comprehensive baseline study and preliminary design of the LIS carried out in 2007–08. The preliminary design of the system proposed a 10-year long-term strategy consisting of two main phases: (1) establishment of the LIS basic infrastructure and (2) enhancement of the LIS system.

### Phase One: Establishment of Uganda's LIS

The overall objective of phase one was to establish the basic LIS infrastructure for the entire country and to transition from a manual land registration service to a computerized one, over an estimated period of seven years. The specific objectives of this phase were simplification and streamlining of the land registration and cadastral procedures, reduction of the cost and time needed for land transactions, and provision of available and affordable land administration services for customers. Phase one was broken down into two stages: (1) a pilot stage for LIS development and testing in six cadastral zonal centers and (2) a roll-out stage. Designed to take three years, the pilot stage aimed to secure existing land records, develop an LIS suitable to local conditions, test the LIS in pilot cadastral zones, and prepare to roll it out to the entire country. The LIS itself was expected to cover land administration, with initial activities focused on land registration and cadastral services. Implementation began in 2010 and ended in February 2013. The roll-out stage, estimated to take four years, aims to expand the LIS to the entire country with a nationwide basic land information infrastructure and with the LIS design enhanced to cover property valuation, physical planning, and support for cadastral surveys; it is expected to start in 2014 with funding from a new World Bank–supported project, which was approved by the World Bank Board in May 2013 (World Bank 2013).

The pilot stage (or pilot), under the responsibility of the MLHUD, was contracted out to a consortium of seven firms. The pilot stage consisted of five main components:

1. Detailed design of the larger national LIS architecture and of the LIS system for piloting in six cadastral zones;
2. Data conversion comprising rehabilitation of the land registers, conversion of registration and cadastral documents to digital form, and preparation of the documentation for system decentralization;
3. Data integration, including integrating the title registration and cadastral data, and identification and recording of technical and other problems in the cadastral and registration data, including incompatibilities and inconsistencies for future resolution;
4. LIS (parcel information management) implementation in the pilot areas including installation and operation of the LIS; and
5. Review of the LIS design and operations to correct any operational problems, to improve system design based on user acceptance tests and lessons learned from the pilot stage, and to prepare a detailed plan for the roll-out stage.

Unlike in Ghana where the different building blocks of LIS were implemented piecemeal, all five components of the LIS pilot in Uganda were implemented under one contract and were very closely coordinated, reducing the risk of systems and subsystems failing to communicate with each other.

### Phase Two: Enhancement of Uganda's LIS

Phase two, due to start in 2014, will enhance and improve the system established in phase one. Its main objective will be to consolidate the results of the first phase, including enhancement of the established infrastructure, extending the LIS to cover property valuation, physical planning, and support to cadastral surveys, and transitioning to an electronic system of land conveyance. The transition to the digital registration system will require additional inputs including the development and enacting of a legislation that recognizes the digital system and establishes the rules of digital registration services. This process is linked to other government initiatives including e-government, greater availability of basic information infrastructure, and provision of more reliable and affordable Internet access. The duration of the second phase will depend on how quickly the enabling legal framework and these other supporting systems and infrastructure can be put in place, but, based on current plans elaborated in the new World Bank–funded project (World Bank 2013), the second phase will start in 2014 and will end in 2019.

### Uganda's LIS Development Approach and Expected Impacts

Based on a vast number of studies,[1] a review of international experience, and consultations with key stakeholders, the preliminary design document for Uganda's LIS suggested options for the broad architecture that articulated advantages and disadvantages, especially for centralized and decentralized approaches, taking into account the following: (1) the large and growing number of districts (among other units) and their implication for establishment, operation, and maintenance costs of the system, (2) the volume of current and projected land transactions, and (3) the accessibility of land administration services to people. Ultimately the government decided to adopt an architectural design that consolidates neighboring districts into 21 cadastral zones. The LIS is being decentralized to zonal centers, but a National Land Information Center will service all of the zonal centers and act as a backup for the land data held at zonal centers.

The LIS system itself consists of three main technologically integrated elements: (1) spatial data management, based on the use of a geographic information system (GIS), (2) a document management system (DMS), and (3) a workflow management system (WMS). These three main elements have already been integrated into one LIS, which, in the initial phase, is mainly limited to parcel information management (Government of Uganda 2007).

The parcel information management system is focused on the management of land records, including cadastral and land registration data. The LIS development work also included the rehabilitation of all existing land titles and instruments as well as cadastral records and maps. The land records were checked, vetted, scanned, and uploaded to the database and linked to appropriate cadastral records. The cadastral maps were digitized and adjusted to the base map imagery processed from ortho-rectified high-resolution satellite imagery and aerial photography. The procedures for all transactions and data updates were managed by the WMS, based on careful mapping and reengineering of existing business processes of land administration. In combination with the DMS, these two systems are responsible for securing land records, and all decisions regarding property transactions can be made only through the system, contributing to the reduction of "back door" practices and cases of fraud that used to be common in the land administration system in Uganda in the recent past.

Agricultural Land Redistribution and Land Administration in Sub-Saharan Africa
http://dx.doi.org/10.1596/978-1-4648-0188-4

Although the first phase of LIS was implemented under the current legal framework, implementation of the second phase will require a change in the existing legal framework. For example, the Survey Act and Registration of Titles Act will need to be updated, and new laws, such as a Digital Signature Law and a Land Information Law, will need to be enacted to allow the use of electronic data. Work on reviewing and drafting these new laws is ongoing, and the necessary amendments and new laws are expected to be ready during implementation of the second phase of LIS. Other ongoing or planned work to complement LIS development includes (1) accelerated formalization of land rights to significantly increase the country's proportion of registered land (currently 18 percent), (2) update and expansion of the national coverage of large-scale base maps, (3) development of a national spatial data infrastructure to facilitate harmonization and sharing of spatial data, and (4) modernization of the national geodetic framework. Some of these activities were partly funded under PSCP II, which closed in February 2013, and will receive continued support under the new World Bank–funded project (World Bank 2013).

Although the implementation of Uganda's LIS is not yet complete, it has already produced some positive impacts, including (1) a decrease in the average time to transfer property, from 227 days in 2007 to 52 days in 2012; (2) a reduction in time to process a mortgage, from several weeks to three days; and (3) a decrease in the number of days to complete a search on an encumbered title, from 15 to 1.

### *Observations and Conclusions from Uganda's LIS Experience*

Uganda's approach to LIS development and implementation was comprehensive, coherent, and all-inclusive, thereby minimizing the risk of future miscommunication between systems or subsystems. It also minimized risks of failure because the development and implementation of the LIS was closely supervised by supervision consultants using an approach similar to that used in engineering projects in the construction industry. But because it did not prioritize quick wins, it faced pressure from political leaders who wanted expedited results. Nevertheless, its early impacts in terms of reducing the time it takes to complete land transactions have been impressive. Work on developing the legal framework for digital technology has begun and will be continued, together with rolling out the pilot LIS, under a follow-up World Bank project. It will take time to roll out the LIS program to cover the whole country, to train the necessary staff, to develop the necessary legal framework to transition to electronic conveyance, and to put in place measures to ensure the availability of financial resources for the system's continued operation and maintenance. The total cost of Phase 1 was about US$11 million, including funding for new large scale maps but excluding funding for new or renovated office buildings. Phase 2 is expected to cost about US$10 million, excluding the costs of new base maps but including costs of new or renovated office buildings. Annual maintenance costs, estimated at 15 percent, would amount to about US$3 million.

Agricultural Land Redistribution and Land Administration in Sub-Saharan Africa
http://dx.doi.org/10.1596/978-1-4648-0188-4

## Challenges and Lessons Learned from Ghana and Uganda's Experiences in Developing LIS

According to the World Bank (2012), SSA countries have been the most active in undertaking reforms: SSA countries undertook 49 reforms to make it easier to register property between 2005 and 2011, compared with a range of 6–34 reforms in other regions of the world. However, their land administration systems are still inefficient. This progress in reforms notwithstanding, more than 80 percent of SSA and South Asian countries still have paper-based systems in deteriorated conditions (World Bank 2012). Hence, developing a computerized LIS is still a largely unfinished business in SSA, and much can be learned from the SSA countries that have made progress in this area.

### Similarities and Differences between Ghana and Uganda's LIS Experiences

In both countries, LIS development is part of a long-term strategy for development of the land sector, as defined by Uganda's 10-year LSSP and Ghana's 15–25-year Land Administration Program. In both countries, LIS implementation is underpinned by long-term financial commitments from development partners.

Development of Uganda's LIS was preceded by and based on a preliminary design, comprehensive terms of reference and technical specifications, and a blueprint for implementation, all prepared upfront to guide detailed design, piloting, and roll-out. The design and piloting were packaged into one major contract, which also included reengineering of business processes and work flows, conversion of cadastral and land records, training of staff, and LIS installation in pilot cadastral zones. Ghana's LIS design and implementation activities were developed with a focus on different elements and subsystems to be integrated later, without the benefit of an upfront architecture design and blueprint to guide implementation. Ghana's approach had the potential benefit of generating early wins, but also the potential risk that the subsystems and other elements could fail to communicate. Last, Uganda's LIS is based on proprietary software, whereas Ghana's LIS is based on FLOSS. The latter is likely to save on annual software fees, but it requires Ghana to develop the local capacity to maintain and update its software programs.

### Potential Issues in LIS Implementation

Based on a review of the progress in LIS development and implementation in Uganda and Ghana, this case study has identified a number of issues that SSA countries should anticipate when undertaking such a task:

- *A lengthy process.* LIS development is a long-term activity, taking up to 10 years, which makes it vulnerable to loss of support unless it is underpinned by strong political commitment and support from development partners. To meet these requirements and to strengthen its feasibility, it is necessary to have a long-term strategy, realistic goals and objectives, and adequate management of stakeholders' expectations. Discontinuation of support for the system during implementation may result in its collapse and lead to an even worse situation than before the system was initiated.

- *Possible resistance, both direct and indirect, to change and power plays by different authorities.* Resistance is probable because LIS implementation requires a deep reengineering of many procedures and established practices, decentralization of decision making, and changes in organizational structures. This may provoke resistance at different levels.

- *Sustainability of project results through capacity development.* LIS implementation requires development of new skills for personnel at different levels to enhance sustainability. Sustainability also requires extensive capacity development to overcome the general technological weaknesses of existing land administration institutions.

- *Outdated legal frameworks in land administration and a low percentage of registered land.* A computerized LIS and electronic conveyance require a new legal framework in many countries. Similarly, a computerized LIS needs to be populated with a critical mass of spatial data, which will require accelerating land registration in most SSA countries.

- *Financial support for operation and maintenance of the computerized LIS.* The LIS needs a noninterruptible electricity supply, skilled and motivated IT personnel, and support for annual licenses for software, hardware maintenance, necessary spare parts, and consumables, as well as for services such as Internet connections. Failure to pay for the provision of such services even for a short time may lead to service disruptions and damages to the system, and finally to the collapse of the system. There is also a reputational risk associated with failing to provide services to customers.

### Lessons Learned from LIS Implementation

Ghana and Uganda are at different stages of LIS system design and implementation, and their final outcomes are not yet known. However, useful lessons can be extracted even at this stage. The lessons emerging from this study are the following:

- LIS development and implementation should be considered an integral part of land administration reform. To the extent that LIS development requires institutional and organizational changes together with changes in the positions and responsibilities of some civil servants working in land administration services, it should also be considered part of public service reforms.

- Development of an LIS is a key driver to improving land administration services and requires a holistic vision, a coherent strategy, and a phased approach to planning and implementation, with buy-in from all key stakeholders.

- Given the technological complexity of LIS projects and the need for high-level expertise that is not always locally available, the development of an LIS should make use of both local knowledge and international expertise, with provisions for contract supervision to advise African clients on whether contract standards and acceptance provisions have been met before contractors are paid for their services.

- Capacity development and training of personnel at all levels of LIS operation and maintenance should be a critical part of LIS development. Capacity development should be directed not only at training on the use of software and hardware but also on the legal and cultural aspects of the work environment. This may be required to transform the attitudes and work habits of public service personnel.

- Development of an LIS requires cooperation between agencies and among different levels of central and local governments.

- Public information and education campaigns at different stages of LIS development are important to get support for the project and to manage expectations. The public outreach campaign should be designed to deliver the message about the advantages of the new system for customers and to get feedback from customers regarding the quality of services provided and areas for improvement.

- The legal framework may need to be updated to accommodate implementation of computerized LIS and to transition to electronic conveyance and other service improvements enabled by ICT.

- LIS development should be based on appropriate modern technology, keeping in mind the rapid changes in technology and the increasing availability and affordability of innovations. Given the variety of affordable solutions and new technologies, it is important that system development be based on demand-driven and user-oriented approaches, not on supply-driven approaches.

- System design requires careful consideration of the different technological approaches such as FLOSS or customer off-the-shelf software. These should be carefully considered from the point of view of maintenance, license payment, system security, and local capacity to operate the system. Maintenance for some period after the LIS has been installed and commissioned should be part of the system design and bid documentation.

- Implementation of an LIS is best done in a sequence, starting with a pilot covering a limited area of the country, and eventually expanding to cover the entire country. It may take seven to ten years to fully implement, including the preliminary design stage.

- Given the critical importance of assured funding for an LIS, from planning and design to full implementation, it is important to secure the government's financial commitment, preferably with donor support.

## Note

1. The studies include those carried out by Greenwood (1990), Larsson (1990), Tibisaasa (1993), Swedesurvey (1996, 2004), Barata (2001), and SiVEST (2003).

## References

Barata, K. 2001. *Rehabilitating Records in the Land Registry*. Final Report. Report written for Chemonics International Inc., USAID/SPEED Project Short Term Consultancy, Kampala, Uganda.

Byamugisha, F. F. K. 2013. *Securing Africa's Land for Shared Prosperity: A Program to Scale Up Reforms and Investments*. Africa Development Forum Series. Washington, DC: World Bank.

Deininger, K., and G. Feder. 2009. "Land Registration, Governance, and Development: Evidence and Implications for Policy." *World Bank Research Observer* 24 (2): 233–66.

Falloux, F. 1989. "Land Information and Remote Sensing for Renewable Resource Management in Sub-Saharan Africa: A Demand-Driven Approach." World Bank Technical Paper 108, World Bank, Washington, DC.

Government of Ghana. 2007. "Terms of Reference for Consultancy Services for Stage One of the Development, Design and Installation of a Land Information System." Ministry of Lands, Forestry and Mines, Accra.

Government of Uganda. 2004. "Land Sector Strategic Plan, 2001–2011: Utilizing Uganda's Land Resources for Sustainable Development." Government of Uganda, Kampala.

———. 2007. *Land Information System Preliminary Design and Architecture*. Final Report, PSCPII. Ministry of Lands, Housing and Urban Development, Kampala.

Greenwood, D. W. 1990. "The Rehabilitation of the Land Survey and Registration in Uganda." Government of Uganda, Kampala.

Hall, G. B., B. A. Quaye, and F. K. Mensah. 2009. *OSCAR Project Report—Ghana*. Accra.

Johnson, S. 2008. *Stage One of the Development, Design and Installation of a Land Information System*. Implementation Strategy Report, Ministry of Lands, Forestry and Mines of Ghana, COWI, Accra.

Larsson, G. 1990. *Rehabilitation and Development of Land Survey and Registration in Uganda*. Consultancy Report, Stockholm.

SiVEST. 2003. *Review of the Status of the Land Information Systems in Uganda*. Project Report, Kampala.

Swedesurvey. 1996. *A Base for a Land Information System in Uganda*. Project Report, Kampala.

———. 2004. *A Concept for National Land Information System in Uganda*. Project Report, Kampala.

Tibisaasa, J. N. 1993. *Rehabilitation and Development of Land Registration System in Uganda*. Report on study tour of Thailand, Hong Kong, Singapore, Queensland, New South Wales, Victoria, South Australia and New Zealand, Ministry of Lands, Water and Environment, Kampala.

UN Economic Commission for Europe. 1996. *Land Administration Guidelines. With Special Reference to Countries in Transition*. United Nations, New York.

World Bank. 2003. "Ghana Land Administration Project." Project Appraisal Document, World Bank, Washington, DC.

———. 2004. "Uganda Second Private Sector Competitiveness Project." Project Appraisal Document, World Bank, Washington, DC.

———. 2011. "Ghana Second Land Administration Project." Project Appraisal Document, World Bank, Washington, DC.

———. 2012. *Doing Business 2012: Doing Business in a More Transparent World*. Washington, DC: World Bank.

———. 2013. "Uganda Competitiveness and Enterprise Development Project." Project Appraisal Document, World Bank, Washington, DC.

World Bank Institute. 2006. "Land Administration in Africa: Searching for Land Tenure Security." World Bank Institute, World Bank, Washington, DC.

# CHAPTER 6

# Inventory of Government Land: Lessons from Ghana and Uganda

Rexford A. Ahene and Frank F. K. Byamugisha

## Introduction

How much land does the government own, and where are its boundaries? Effective management of land, including its use to produce public goods such as infrastructure, its use by public bodies such as schools and security agencies, or its allocation for use by investors or land-poor farmers, is almost impossible unless these two questions can be answered. The ability to answer these questions requires having a detailed inventory of public land and its boundaries as well as its current occupiers and uses. Most countries in Sub-Saharan Africa (SSA) currently do not have that spatial and ownership information and thus need to undertake inventories of their public land. This case study reviews Ghana and Uganda's recent efforts to address this problem. With support from the World Bank, both countries undertook systematic (as opposed to sporadic) land inventories of state-acquired and occupied lands; these represent the most recent attempts in SSA to accurately account for such land.[1]

Ghana and Uganda are good case studies in the context of SSA given that both countries have a checkered and predominantly unfavorable history of compulsory alienation of land rights under the guise of the public interest before and after their respective independences. In both countries, accumulated government-owned or publicly vested lands are a source of continuing tension between the state, current occupants, and former inadequately compensated landowners, and the situation is aggravated by delayed payment of outstanding compensation to former owners. Other issues include nonutilization of all or part of the acquired land, various degrees of encroachment on acquired sites, and unauthorized changes in the use or disposition of parts of the acquired parcels. These patterns of mismanagement were found by the governments of Ghana and Uganda to be systemic enough to require a holistic examination of existing policy and practices to improve the management of government-acquired and vested land and the associated real estate assets.

To date, Ghana has been more successful in undertaking a systematic and substantial inventory of its state lands; Uganda has only done so more recently and on a more limited scale. Ghana's land inventory exercises, initiated in 2003, had two objectives: (1) to enable land sector agencies to obtain up-to-date and accurate records on all government-acquired and occupied lands, and (2) to enable the government to formulate and implement policy guidelines on compulsory acquisitions, compensation, and divestiture of public lands no longer needed for their intended public purpose (World Bank 2003). About 60 percent of Ghana's estimated public lands were included in the inventory exercises, which provided a clearer picture of the principal sources of tension in communities impacted by government land acquisitions. The inventory also helped the government to issue short-term policy guidelines for managing state land assets while waiting for information from the whole country inventory. In contrast, Uganda's land inventory exercise, conducted from 2009 to 2011, covered only 10 percent of state lands and was faced with design and implementation problems that are being corrected before resuming the exercise under a follow-up project (World Bank 2013). The objectives of the land inventory in Uganda has been to identify, survey, confirm ownership, and determine the status of occupation of land with a view to determining the most appropriate policy and legal framework to underpin its optimal management and use (World Bank 2005).

## Objectives of the Case Study

The objective of this case study is to draw lessons from Ghana and Uganda's land inventory experiences to inform future work in this area in these countries and in others that may eventually undertake land inventories. Lessons of interest include those from the design and implementation of the land inventories as well as those on the use of the data generated to inform policies and actions to improve public land management. The case study is based on a review of relevant documents produced from the land inventory exercises, especially survey and valuation reports, as well as on interviews with relevant government officials and consultants involved in the exercises. The lessons learned are expected to enhance the processes of inventory acquisition and to improve the quality and reliability of the collected cadastral data and land use information; the latter should help improve policy development and implementation to better manage the stock of government-owned and vested lands and to dispose of surplus lands to investors and land-poor farmers more efficiently and equitably.

## Historical Background

The government of Ghana launched a new Land Policy in June 1999 with the long-term policy goals of promoting social stability, improving security of land tenure, and simplifying the process for fair, transparent, and efficient administration of land. The development goal was to provide a framework for stimulating economic development and reducing poverty. To pursue this, the government secured the assistance of the World Bank and other development partners and launched a 15–25-year Land Administration Program in October 2003 (World Bank 2003). The first five years of the associated Land Administration Project (LAP-1) focused on developing a new infrastructure and technology platform for a sustainable land administration system that would be efficient, decentralized, and capable of supporting implementation of the new Land Policy and providing a "one-stop-shop" land administration framework.

In Uganda the scenario leading to the land inventory exercise was similar to that in Ghana. After approving a new constitution in 1995 with significant provisions on land, and a new 1998 Land Act thereafter, the government of Uganda prepared a 10-year Land Sector Strategic Plan (2001–11). The LSSP was to guide implementation of the land provisions of the new constitution and the 1998 Land Act (Government of Uganda 2001). The government of Uganda approved a comprehensive inventory of government land to support its improved management as one of the activities funded under the Second Private Sector Competitiveness Project (PSCP II), supported by the World Bank (2004).

## Institutional Challenges to Inventorying Government Land

Planning and implementing a land inventory is challenging. Given the considerable level of corruption and mismanagement associated with government land, it takes political will and pressure against vested interests to mobilize resources and embark on a government land inventory meant to eradicate those vices (Mabogunje 1992). Another challenge is the incursion of central government powers into matters pertaining to autonomy over public property held by lower tier governments, ministries, departments, and statutory bodies, and the need to reform entrenched attitudes to improve accountability over such land assets.

Lack of transparency in government land transactions is not restricted to African and developing countries. Questionable dealings, "insider" transfers, secretive rezoning of land parcels, and other abuses are a common element of land transactions worldwide. Transfer of development rights through political processes not subject to scrutiny, transparency, and accountability have been found to permeate public sector procedures for property disposal, and income from corrupted property allocations represents a significant source of illicit payments in many countries. However, these challenges are not insurmountable if a central government is committed to promoting transparency and good governance.

## Defining Government Land

Government land in both Ghana and Uganda comprises land that is occupied and used by the government for public purposes or reserved for future use by the government, plus land held in trust on behalf of the wider public. This definition includes land occupied by government offices, schools, hospitals, police stations, prisons, and military installations, land on which social infrastructure is located,

Agricultural Land Redistribution and Land Administration in Sub-Saharan Africa
http://dx.doi.org/10.1596/978-1-4648-0188-4

and land owned but not used or occupied by the government. For the purpose of this case study, government land is limited to that owned by either the central or local governments.

The principal difference between government and private land is that the public sector must recognize the public interest and the constitutionality of its obligations. The public interest may be reflected in a gazette notice or an executive instrument authorizing the acquisition and may include a broad array of activities, such as construction of public infrastructure; provision of education and health facilities, national parks and conservation areas, military facilities, and state, regional, and local government offices; the undertaking of urban development or redevelopment schemes; and establishment and operation of public parks. However, in addition to these clearly designated government land acquisitions, several other instances can be identified where allodial landowners, private institutions and churches, or local community leaders have formally or informally granted land for public use and operation as public facilities, requiring no payment of compensation by the government and without any formal documentation of the deed of gift. This class of government lands is the most likely to be subject to contradictory interpretations of original intent in the future.

The current legal frameworks in Ghana and Uganda are more focused on protecting the acquisition and ownership of lands by the government, and less on their management and upkeep or the possibility of deriving economic benefits from them. Similarly, the governments' decision-making processes lean more toward protection of property rights than better management of land assets. In fact, the law in both countries provides guidelines to prevent the disposal of government lands as long as they are needed for public purposes. Yet on the whole, despite the unquestionably high public interest in government land and real estate assets, questions arise when excess land or underutilization of acquired lands exists, because this reflects symptoms of poor management.

## Institutional Framework for Government Land Administration

The Lands Commission in Ghana and the Uganda Land Commission (ULC) have constitutional mandates to act on behalf of the government and to manage public lands and any other lands vested in the state or the Commissions. However, in Ghana the Lands Commission Act of 2008 (Act 767) also consolidated the mandate to include all land administration matters. The goal was to promote a "one-stop-shop" approach to land administration and the judicious use of land by society and to ensure that land is used to achieve development goals. To fulfill this broader mission, Ghana's Land Commission collaborates closely on land management decisions with (1) the Office of the Administrator of Stool Lands, (2) the department responsible for town and country planning, (3) structures designed for the customary administration of stool, skin, family- or community-owned land, or any other land, and (4) other public agencies, government bodies, and any other private body that has operations or activities relevant to the functions of the Commission.[2]

Similarly, ULC in Uganda is the custodian of all land assets owned by the national government. ULC also advises central government agencies, local authorities, and traditional leaders on the policy framework for development of land they occupy and is the principal agency authorized to allocate and/or divest government land for public and private use and occupation. Certain categories of land, such as road reserves, forest reserves, wildlife reserves, conservation areas, and wetlands, are managed by authorized statutory agencies of the government, with a clearly defined mission and legal and administrative mandates.

## The Challenge of Land Valuation and Compensation

With their wide range of functions and services, Ghana and Uganda's public sectors have accumulated a very large and diversified portfolio of land, making them the largest land and real property owner in both countries. Not only is the value of government land assets enormous, but so are the costs associated with their effective management and protection, as well as the costs of resolving outstanding compensation claims. Optimizing the management of government land by developing an accurate inventory should result in significant savings to the government.

Tools for asset valuation, efficient utilization, and determining optimal disposal of land are available, but the political will to apply them in a transparent and consistent manner is not. Often there is political interference in the day-to-day work of the commissions. Well-conducted land inventories would help generate the necessary information to increase transparency, consistency, effectiveness, and efficiency in the management of land by the agencies that have been entrusted to manage the government land.

## Acquisition and Disposal of Land by the Government

The application of a state's power of eminent domain, principally through compulsory acquisition or occupation, often creates problems between the state and the expropriated owners. In Uganda the central government or local government can acquire land by compulsory acquisition under the police powers of the state. The procedure for such acquisition is governed by legislation. However, in addition to legal processes, government and statutory corporations, including ULC and District Land Boards (DLBs), can acquire land through tenancies, leases, and purchase under any of the statutorily recognized land tenure categories. No specific law regulates the contracts for land acquisition by the central government, local governments, or statutory corporations in both Ghana and Uganda. The practice has been to negotiate privately with vendors without having to follow the bidding and other competitive procedures required by the Public Procurement and Disposal of Public Assets laws in Ghana or Uganda. Such acquisitions are governed only by financial regulations on the use of funds by public authorities.

Agricultural Land Redistribution and Land Administration in Sub-Saharan Africa
http://dx.doi.org/10.1596/978-1-4648-0188-4

Regarding the disposal of land vested in ULC or municipal councils, previous guidelines in Uganda required this to be done under statutory leases.[3] The absence of legal requirements for regulating the disposal of government land and real estate assets left much to the discretion of ULC and the municipal councils, including whether to advertise or sell the land by competitive means, as is required in many countries.[4] The current practice is for ULC and DLBs in Uganda to act as if they are still making grants. The Ghana Land Commission and its Regional Land Offices act the same way.

Similarly, the disposal of land by local governments and statutory corporations is equally unregulated in both Ghana and Uganda. In most cases, tenancies, leases, and sales are not made under a competitive and transparent process that ensures that land is disposed for value. Consequently, inefficiencies in the form of physical and economic underutilization and insufficient monitoring, maintenance, and protection stem from the fundamental belief that land and real property held by government are free goods, owned by taxpayers, and not subject to the same economic rationalization that occurs in private ownership. In such circumstances, it is difficult, if not impossible, to measure the economic loss due to poor management and the inability to account for the stock and condition of government land. Lack of information creates multiple inefficiencies that may be attributed to the large amount of underutilized land held by government departments and agencies whose needs change faster than their ability to reuse or dispose of excess properties. This makes such government land assets a de facto liability in the affected communities, since the cost of holding these land assets is neither emphasized nor accounted for and there is therefore no incentive or financial benefit to relinquish them.

## Common Purpose of a Government Land Inventory

The general paucity of information on government land and real property is a significant issue in SSA. According to Kaganova and McKellar (2006), only a few countries have computerized land information systems capable of generating a comprehensive inventory of government-owned land and buildings. Even the most advanced industrialized countries, including New Zealand, the United Kingdom, and the United States, had inconsistent inventory records of government-owned land and buildings as late as 2002. Although significant improvements in the quality of inventory data have occurred since then, government land and property inventory deficiencies are still the norm in most places (Kaganova and McKellar 2006). Apart from the actual number of holdings, the most conspicuous gaps include data on historic significance, utilization status or situation analysis, inventory of in-and-out leases, and reliable financial information for tracking revenues and expenses. Potential market value is frequently unknown, and the availability of information on legal status is often spotty. Detailed record keeping is essential to cope with disputes, ascertain market trends, determine values, and compare performance against public sector objective benchmarks.

Often some of the primary outputs from the maps and attribute information collected in an inventory of government land are the following:

- Baseline data on the location, size, and features of government land;
- Comprehensive management plans;
- Identification of government land for development;
- Identification of government land for education and social infrastructure;
- Evaluations or functional assessments of government land;
- Environmental impact assessments;
- Site selection for public infrastructure corridors (e.g., power lines);
- Analysis of forestry, conservation, and wildlife habitat policies.

Furthermore, to disseminate inventory information once it is created, the appropriate land sector agencies can create several products, such as the following:

- Maps in printed and digital format;
- Government land inventory reports;
- Government land utilization status reports;
- Government land values databases.

With thousands of acres and thousands of government buildings, parks, and reserves in the government land portfolios in both Ghana and Uganda, it is imperative to identify what the government owns, to determine whether government, community, or private ownership is most effective, and to streamline the equitable and efficient transfer of all unneeded land to communities or investors.

## Conducting a Government Land Inventory in Ghana and Uganda

This section covers three key elements that underpinned the conduct of the government land inventories in Ghana and Uganda: (1) the rationale for the exercise, (2) the objectives of the exercise, and (3) the key steps involved in the exercise.

### Rationale for Conducting Government Land Inventories

For Uganda and Ghana, the main rationale of conducting a government land inventory was to identify government land and to generate necessary information to improve its management. For Ghana, a long outstanding need was developing a policy to address delayed or lack of payment of compensation for postindependence land acquisitions of lands under the trust of traditional chiefs and clan heads. This required information on the location, size, value, and occupation status of such lands in addition to identifying former owners. For Uganda, the urgency for a government land inventory was to establish precisely the amount of land owned by the state and to confirm the ownership with a view to determine availability of surplus land that could be allocated to the landless poor and investors.

Agricultural Land Redistribution and Land Administration in Sub-Saharan Africa
http://dx.doi.org/10.1596/978-1-4648-0188-4

## Objectives of a Government Land Inventory

The overall objective of the inventory exercise in both countries was to enable the government to formulate and implement realistic policies on state-acquired and -occupied lands. The immediate practical emphasis in Uganda was to account for the stock of state or public lands as a clearly distinguishable ownership category in its National Land Information System. The ultimate goal was to ensure that all government land was surveyed and titled to the state and clearly distinguished from private land as a measure to protect government land assets and to manage them efficiently.

The specific objectives of Ghana's inventory exercise, as stated in the LAP (World Bank 2003), were to do the following:

• Ascertain the stock of state or public lands including the effective usage of such lands; these include lands that have either been compulsorily acquired or occupied by the state without formal acquisition;
• Ascertain the instruments that were used for the acquisition as well as to determine how the state occupied the lands without any formal acquisition;
• Identify the boundaries of the acquired lands; this shall include the determination of the extent of acquisition as indicated in the cadastral/certified/land development plan, and to ascertain the actual area occupied by the beneficiaries, unoccupied areas and the method of protection of the boundaries, and where there are no plans, landmarks used by the occupiers for the identification of the boundaries shall be indicated;
• Determine the acquisitions for which compensation has been paid and those for which partial or no compensation has been paid;
• Determine the quantum of outstanding compensation;
• Ascertain acquisitions for which there has been change of use as against the original purpose of the acquisition; and
• Assess the extent of encroachment (if any) on the acquired or occupied lands.

These objectives illustrate that Ghana is moving to distinguish its land assets not by the nature of the appropriation, but according to ownership. The move also adds transparency by placing into a specific public portfolio government land assets that are exclusively dedicated to public use and thus governed by special legal and institutional procedures aimed at protecting such land assets against unauthorized use, encroachment, and mismanagement.

## Key Steps to Undertaking a Land Inventory

The design and development of any land inventory system is a difficult, long-term undertaking that calls for careful planning, attention to methodological details, and sustained financial and technical capacity to execute and utilize the information collected after the initial compilation is over. As observed by Aronoff (1990), experiences in other countries, including Botswana, have shown that problems associated with people are almost always the most significant obstacle to successful implementation of a land inventory system. After the decision to develop an inventory is made, several requirements for designing and responding to the needs and concerns that initially prompted the development of the inventory have to be identified and carefully defined as analytical requirements.

Key steps taken in the government land inventory processes used in Ghana and Uganda included the following major activities, described in more detail in the following sections:

- Preliminary scoping and workload assessment;
- Compilation of existing data and methodological refinements;
- Sustained communication and awareness campaign;
- Technically sound and cost-effective execution of field work.

### Preliminary Scoping and Workload Assessment

Preliminary scoping is important for clarifying user requirements, examining the appropriateness of the methodology, and determining technical and administrative capacity requirements and potential budgeting needs. In addition, information gaps discovered during scoping help to sharpen the terms of reference, the scope of work, and the performance obligations of both the public and private sector participants in the inventory exercise.

For the Uganda land inventory, the activities undertaken during the scoping study, aptly described as an "Assessment of Workload Study," included the following:

- Assembling the project team, which consisted of key players in the Land Administration division of Uganda's Ministry of Lands, Housing and Urban Development, the Digital Mapping Unit of the Surveys and Mapping Department, and a private survey firm as consultants;
- Reviewing existing functions and processes at every stage of the land title registration process and determining which new applications would be required;
- Making an initial assessment of the workload.

The scoping exercise in Uganda was instrumental in providing sample data for projecting the mean workload for each district and rough projections for a comprehensive national land inventory. Where possible, interviews were conducted with stakeholders, for example, with land managers of the districts, local administrators, relevant technocrats, knowledgeable elders, and locals in the proximity of the land parcel. The "Assessment of Workload Study" also served as a pilot training program for the land sector agencies and private contractors who were expected to play complementary roles during implementation. Building capacity in the private sector had the added advantage of enabling private firms to play a more active role in delivering land services at the local level.

The nature of engagement with stakeholders, including traditional authorities and local political leadership, the communication and awareness creation, and other lessons learned during the assessment exercise, enabled guidelines for the inventory exercise to be developed. The information gathered was also used to develop a standardized data collection form for organizing field data for each land parcel detailing the location of the parcel, the tenure status, current and/or planned land use, level and nature of encroachment, and people's attitudes toward ownership and utilization.

### Compilation of Existing Information and Methodological Refinements

The absence of reliable information is a fundamental reason for conducting an inventory, but the primary decision of whether to undertake an inventory depends on the types of questions the inventory is expected to answer. For example, in Ghana, prior to the consolidation of all land administration agencies under the new Lands Commission in 2009, government land information was held by the old Lands Commission and three other public sector land agencies, namely, the Land Valuation Board, the Survey Department, and the Town and Country Planning Department. Most of the information had not been updated for years, and in some cases, the records could not be found. Consequently, neither the total number of acquisitions—complete and incomplete—nor the extent of development could be ascertained. There was no comprehensive record of all the government land and the developments on it.

The methodology for conducting the inventory had five distinct steps:

- Desktop research including review and compilation of existing documents;
- An assessment of the pilot workload and development of guidelines (including a manual and a diary of activities);
- Communication and awareness creation including sensitization workshops;
- Field activity by survey teams, valuers, land officers, and planners;
- Data analysis and continuous user acceptance reviews.

In the Uganda government inventory, land officers with extensive experience in compulsory acquisition schedules were deployed in three teams to compile the list of acquired lands and prepare proprietary and acquisition plans for the field work. Desktop research and additional information revealed during the sensitization workshops were made available to the private sector consultants.

A broad consultation exercise was undertaken with several government ministries and departments, local government, DLBs, statutory corporations, and agencies to generate an initial list of government land. However, to ensure completeness, this list was reviewed and reconciled with a second checklist developed by community leaders, traditional authorities, and local residents and certified by local administrators. This approach helped to account for local parcels that may have been missed by the public sector agencies.

### Communication and Awareness Creation Campaign

A key to the success of a land inventory lies in the creation of effective public awareness and sensitization of all stakeholders. Communication and awareness creation are essential to inform the public and to ensure the safety of contractors. The awareness step also provides an early opportunity to explore system development questions, such as: What land inventory system to develop? Which agencies should participate in the development of the system? How and why is public participation important throughout the inventory development process? (Wagner 2009). Typical communication and public awareness tools include the following:

- Fliers explaining the exercise;
- Radio discussions;
- Documentaries for television and other audiovisual broadcasts;
- TV discussions;
- Public information dissemination by Information, Education and Communication Services divisions;
- Timely newspaper adverts and feature articles;
- Interactions with police, traditional authorities, and other related institutions;
- Public meetings, workshops, and press conferences.

Experience has shown that communication campaigns should always be a public sector activity led by multidisciplinary teams. They should involve different strategies and tools to facilitate access to the community and to elicit the cooperation of local stakeholders. The inventory exercises in Ghana and Uganda included a rapid response component to the implementation teams to further ensure quality, to improve communication links with the public sector agencies, and to resolve any potential problems in a timely fashion. In Ghana, at least two officers from the land sector agencies (one of whom was a land surveyor) were attached to each private contractor and paid a daily subsistence allowance (DSA) from the project's operational funds. In Uganda, on the other hand, a special committee of government officers (composed of a land surveyor, a land administrator, a geographic information system (GIS) specialist, and a social economist) served as a "rapid response" link between the contractor and the government to address implementation issues and contract execution challenges without delay. However, because its members were not embedded with the field team, failure to promptly communicate problems and botched attempts by the contractor to independently resolve challenges in the field politicized some problems, escalated public animosity toward the inventory exercise, and limited its success.

### Execution of Field Work
The public sector took the lead role in the inventory exercise in both Ghana and Uganda to perform the following actions:

- Provide access to data held in public agencies' records;
- Engage with local political leadership and traditional authorities to create access for the contractors;
- Communicate and raise awareness;
- Provide quality control and supervision.

Agricultural Land Redistribution and Land Administration in Sub-Saharan Africa
http://dx.doi.org/10.1596/978-1-4648-0188-4

In both countries, private sector contractors were responsible for the following:

- Collection of field data;
- Data analysis and report writing;
- Application and all supporting documents for registration and titling of previously unregistered government land.

Private contractors conducted the pilot land inventory in selected districts in each country. This allowed the methodologies and strategies to be tested before scaling up. Additional orientation and training was organized for interested firms, including practical field work with the field officers from the public sector. The public sector support and quality control role was also tested and refined.

Contractors were given access to data held by the following public sector agencies (in all cases, private properties occupied by state and parastatal agencies were excluded from the inventory):

- The ULC in Uganda;
- The Lands Commission in Ghana including the Survey, Valuation and Registration Divisions;
- The Survey Department and the Valuation Division in Uganda;
- The Land Registries in Uganda (leasehold, freehold, and *mailo*);
- Town and Country Planning Departments in both Uganda and Ghana;
- District Assemblies in Ghana and District Councils in Uganda;
- Ministries and municipalities in both Uganda and Ghana.

The actual field work comprised surveying, updating the status of land use, and conducting valuation activities. In Ghana, contracted firms were required to use predesigned LAP forms to capture and analyze the relevant data. Although a similar data capture template was provided in Uganda, the contractor chose to use its own format and software, making it extremely difficult for the Survey Department to check and approve the results.[5] In both countries the data captured for each parcel of government land for each of the three major activities can be summarized as follows:[6]

1. Surveying
   - Identify and demarcate boundaries.
   - Determine acreage:
     - Total land acquired;
     - Extent of development for the intended purpose;
     - Undeveloped portion;
     - Area encroached upon (if any); and
     - Change of use by beneficiary government agency (if any).
   - Provide points of departure to the required survey standards on each site.
   - Produce provisional survey plans for sites without plans with the use of GPS.

2. Land use information
  - Where there is a planning scheme, indicate whether development does or does not conform.
  - Indicate where there are no schemes and state the dominant land use.
  - Indicate the state, nature, and source of encroachments.
  - Take terrestrial photography of important and/or interesting landmarks.

3. Valuation
  - Discuss evidence of values with management of the Land Valuation Board before submission of draft valuation report.
  - Determine compensable values and submit draft valuation reports after consultation with the Land Valuation Board in situations where compensation has not been paid and where acquisition is incomplete (i.e., state occupied sites).
  - Take terrestrial photographs where necessary (i.e., photographs of sites of massive encroachments, vast undeveloped portions, etc., of the acquired/occupied sites).

In both countries, the exercise was expected to achieve the following outputs:

- A well-informed public, fully sensitized to the government's intentions in undertaking the inventory exercise;
- Up-to-date data sets on state-acquired and -occupied lands;
- Enhanced capacity of both the public and private sectors;
- Reports on the inventory exercise available to all user agencies.

## Institutional Weaknesses in Managing the Uganda Inventory

Considerable weaknesses were present in the conducting of the government land inventory in Uganda, partly because of institutional weaknesses in government to supervise and manage the exercise. Symptoms of these weaknesses could even be seen from the status of formalization of government ownership of the various land parcels claimed by government from the scoping exercise before the inventory itself started. Many of the land parcels were far from reaching the final stage of registration, with many of them either surveyed and not titled, not surveyed though gazetted, and neither surveyed nor gazetted. The incompleteness of the formalization of ownership of land claimed by government pointed to a need to review the functions and technical capabilities of the agencies directly responsible for identifying, gazetting, surveying, and registering government land. The analysis revealed that both the ULC (the authorized body that owns and manages land on behalf of the central government) and the DLBs (which administer land on behalf of the local government) lacked the professional and technical capacity for processing the information generated to complete the inventory.

Further analysis of the steps mandated by law for conducting and approving cadastral surveys identified other bottlenecks including critical staff shortages at every stage of the process, inadequate geodetic controls, and general lack of technical capacity in District Land Offices. These limitations made it difficult for these agencies to monitor the contractor's survey teams in the field and contributed to significant delays in the approval of survey data presented by the contractor. In several documented instances, the private contractor was forced to supply the software for checking the contractor's outputs and the stationery required by District Land Offices to produce deed plans just to complete that stage of the exercise.

## Financial Arrangements

In the case of the public sector–led pilot in Ghana, LAP funding covered four teams of field officers—two of them consisting of only land surveyors and the other two comprising valuers, land officers, and planners—to conduct the field activities under the direct supervision of a task leader in the time frame established.[7] Each site was first visited by the surveying teams who, in addition to their demarcation responsibilities, were also responsible for securing access to each site. This paved the way for the land administration teams to follow. The private consultants were also advised to follow the same model and to use predesigned field data capture forms to organize the data captured and to facilitate analysis.

The LAP Unit in Ghana was responsible for facilitating the payment of all monies required for the exercise upon the receipt of an approved budget from the lead implementing agency. In the case of the private consultants, their payments were made upon satisfactory delivery of outputs as outlined in their contract.

Similarly, PSCP II in Uganda provided the funding for engaging the services of a single contractor selected through international competitive bidding, but was reluctant to provide funding for the public sector staff responsible for monitoring and quality assurance or for members of the Technical Link Committee to visit sites for inspections. The Land Act in Uganda, for example, stipulates that Area Land Committee members have to observe and approve all demarcations for cadastral surveys in their jurisdiction. Furthermore, the contractor's data have to be checked by the District Surveyor before deed plans can be presented to the DLB for consent to register. Unfortunately, the normal annual budgets for Area Land Committees and DLBs were not adequate to handle the exponential increase in activity generated by the inventory exercise, and no supplemental funding was provided by PSCP II or the contractor. In the end, the poor performance of the Uganda exercise was partially attributed to inadequate supervision and delayed interventions to resolve bottlenecks and unexpected challenges.

## Lessons Learned

According to seminal work by Crain and MacDonald (1984), the compilation of a land inventory is only the first stage of a three-tiered integrated land information system (LIS). The other two stages, analysis applications and management applications, are currently being developed as part of a parcel-based LIS in both Ghana and Uganda (see chapter 5). However, the experiences there have shown that there are no easy, ready-made solutions available, hence the need for careful strategic planning, learning from past experiences, and building capacity to manage and sustain the systems built. Just developing an inventory is not sufficient. The integrated LIS has to be supported and continuously updated to ensure its reliability, and staff must be trained to monitor, sustain, and improve the system for it to achieve its intended policy and national development objectives.

At least seven lessons can be drawn from Ghana and Uganda's experiences with land inventory exercises:

- The methodology to identify government land parcels in each district should allow public verification of independently generated lists of government land from various sources before arriving at the final approved list of government land in each district.

- When special projects such as land inventories are being implemented, the capacity at the district level should be augmented to handle the additional work load. Arrangements should include (1) a dedicated amount of time to accompany the contractor in the field, (2) elimination of the backlog of office work created as a result of the demands of the inventory project, and (3) accommodations for the volume of additional work generated (computing, plotting, and preparation of deed plans).

- A public-private partnership (PPP) arrangement (as was used in Ghana) seems to be more appropriate than either a purely public or private arrangement for conducting land inventory projects. It is necessary to provide extra facilitation in the form of DSAs for public sector employees at all levels of government, as well as targeted technical support and additional human resources to facilitate data handling, information processing, and analysis at all stages of the process, especially at regional and central government levels to avoid inordinate delays in completing the project.

- The use of manual records for operational purposes in the land offices is costly, inefficient, and unlikely to meet the land information needs of the user departments and the society at large. Thus there is a need to modernize routine administration and land management functions, particularly the processing of applications for land allocation and approval of consent to register land by Land Boards.

- Land inventory contracts should be awarded only with an agreed upon approach for specifying the actual number of parcels to be surveyed in each lot by the contractor. An acceptable margin of error should be established to guide negotiations once the activity is under way. In addition, establishing clear criteria for determining changes in the scope of work, such as the discovery of additional government land parcels in the course of the activity, would help not only in improving contract management but also in establishing predictable budget ceilings for the activity.

- The participation of public officials whose role in executing the land inventory is considered indispensable, especially if mandated by law, should be planned for and financed to ensure capacity limitations do not become an insurmountable bottleneck to project completion. The nature of the public-private interface mandated by existing laws for executing any land demarcation and registration exercise should be defined to ensure that adequate capacity exists for successful execution of the contract.

- The source and magnitude of the financial, technical, and material resources required to support all aspects of the land inventory should be clearly indicated, and budget lines established for each activity phase. The time frame for execution of the contract should be adhered to, with positive as well as punitive incentives built in to ensure all parties comply with the delivery timelines established for each stage of the activity.

Using a PPP, the land inventory can be structured in three stages to ensure a timely and uninterrupted execution:

*Stage I:* A team of officials appointed by the lead central land agency, working with land officials at lower levels of government, should be charged with identifying and preparing a comprehensive list of government land to be included in the inventory on a district-by-district basis. The number of parcels identified for each district should provide a certified list of plots upon which to base the contract prices and implementation budget requirements for each district. It is also important to establish a per-parcel delivered price range, possibly based on standardized parcel attributes, to guide bidders. Public awareness, sensitization, and training activities should be placed exclusively in the hands of a carefully appointed interdisciplinary team of public and private sector professional and technical specialists. This team should take full responsibility for the training of public sector participants at the national, regional, and district levels, and for raising the awareness and sensitizing stakeholders in the private sector and local communities. This team should also train and orient all key participants throughout the inventory process.

*Stage II:* The adjudication, demarcation, and preparation of sketch maps, surveying and computation, geo-referencing and plotting of the data collected, and preparation of registration plans and applications should be contracted out to private survey firms. The deliverables from this stage include (1) approved field survey data presented in a form prescribed by the receiving public sector department; (2) updated district cadastral index maps; (3) government land situation analysis reports indicating the level of encroachment, land use, improvements, and other specified user requirements; and (4) approved applications for titles and the accompanying approved deed plans.

Agricultural Land Redistribution and Land Administration in Sub-Saharan Africa
http://dx.doi.org/10.1596/978-1-4648-0188-4

*Stage III:* The results of the district-level operations should be transferred to the Survey and Mapping Division at the central government level for final checking. These should later be transferred to the Land Administration Department and finally to the Commissioner for Land Registration, who should issue the titles. These Stage III activities are required by law to be performed by authorized government officers and cannot be delegated to private contractors. Thus the private contractor should submit all required information to the appropriate public sector agency for final processing.

## Conclusions

This case study has highlighted the similarities of and differences between Ghana and Uganda's efforts to develop and implement government land inventory systems. Given the impetus from recent institutional reforms in both countries, the development of new land information management technologies capable of supporting land inventory systems has made it imperative for Ghana and Uganda to verify the status of government lands as a springboard to improving their management. Although both countries faced considerable challenges in their initial attempts, the experience provided valuable lessons that can inform a more realistic approach in their next attempt. The experience can also inform other SSA countries preparing for similar exercises.

Overall, this case study found that in addition to addressing capacity constraints, measures are needed to deal with overarching fundamental land policy and land administration issues, particularly those related to the legal framework, land valuation, and outstanding compensation payments. Finally, there is a clear need to ensure that the land inventory system is planned in conjunction with the development of integrated land information management systems.

## Notes

1. The most comprehensive attempt at developing a comprehensive land inventory system in SSA prior to the attempts in Ghana and Uganda was in Botswana (Government of Botswana 1995; UN-Habitat 2010).

2. "Stool or skin lands are community lands vested in the traditional chief or other community leaders on behalf of the tribe" (Kuntu-Mensah 2006, 3).

3. See Sections 17–38 of the now repealed Public Land Act, 1969 (Government of Uganda 1969).

4. The standard legal requirement in many countries is to advertise the land and sell it by competitive bidding. See Government of Malta (2004), Government of Kenya (1984), and Government of Mauritius (1982).

5. Direct communication with the Director of Lands Department in Uganda's Ministry of Lands, Housing and Urban Development.

6. See guidelines for the inventory exercise in Ghana (Government of Ghana 2007).

7. Field work comprising surveying, valuation, land management, and land use planning activities was undertaken from September 1, 2004, to December 19, 2005.

# References

Aronoff, S. 1990. *Geographic Information Systems: A Management Perspective*. Ottawa: WDL Publications.

Crain, I. K., and C. L. MacDonald. 1984. "From Land Inventory to Land Management." *Cartographica* 21: 40–60.

Government of Botswana, Ministry of Local Government, Lands and Housing. 1995. *Land Inventory for Tribal Areas of Botswana*. Final Report, Ministry Task Force on Land Inventory, Gaborone.

Government of Ghana. 2007. "Guidelines for Private Participation: Inventory of State Acquired and Occupied Lands." Land Administration Project, Ministry of Lands, Forestry and Mines, Accra.

Government of Kenya. 1984. *Government Lands Act, Cap. 280 (revised)*. Nairobi.

Government of Malta. 2004. "Disposal of Government Land Act, Cap. 268 (as amended 2004)." Government of Malta, Valletta.

Government of Mauritius. 1982. "State Lands Act, Rl 2/183/1982." Government of Mauritius, Port Louis.

Government of Uganda. 1969. *Public Land Act, 1969*. Kampala: Government of Uganda.

———. 2001. "Land Sector Strategic Plan 2001–2011: Utilizing Uganda's Land Resources for Sustainable, Pro-Poor Development." Ministry of Water, Lands and Environment, Kampala.

Kaganova, O., and J. McKellar. 2006. *Managing Government Property Assets: International Experiences*. Washington, DC: Urban Institute Press.

Kuntu-Mensah, P. 2006. *On the Implementation of Land Title Registration in Ghana*. Promoting Land Administration and Good Governance, 5th FIG Regional Conference, Accra, Ghana, March 8–11. http://www.fig.net/pub/accra/papers/ts14/ts14_03 _kuntumensah.pdf.

Mabogunje, A. L. 1992. "Perspectives on Urban Land and Urban Management Policies in Sub-Saharan Africa." Technical Paper 196, Africa Technical Department Series, World Bank, Washington, DC.

UN-Habitat. 2010. *Land Inventory in Botswana: Processes and Lessons*. United Nations Human Settlements Program, Nairobi.

Wagner, R. 2009. *How to Implement a Land Inventory*. UN-Habitat, Nairobi.

World Bank. 2003. "Ghana Land Administration Project." Project Appraisal Document, World Bank, Washington, DC.

———. 2004. "Uganda Second Private Sector Competitiveness Project." Project Appraisal Document, World Bank, Washington, DC.

———. 2005. *Uganda Second Private Sector Competitiveness Project, Land Component Project Implementation Manual*. World Bank, Washington, DC.

———. 2013. "Uganda Competitiveness and Enterprise Development Project." Project Appraisal Document, World Bank, Washington, DC.

## Environmental Benefits Statement

The World Bank Group is committed to reducing its environmental footprint. In support of this commitment, the Publishing and Knowledge Division leverages electronic publishing options and print-on-demand technology, which is located in regional hubs worldwide. Together, these initiatives enable print runs to be lowered and shipping distances decreased, resulting in reduced paper consumption, chemical use, greenhouse gas emissions, and waste.

The Publishing and Knowledge Division follows the recommended standards for paper use set by the Green Press Initiative. Whenever possible, books are printed on 50 percent to 100 percent postconsumer recycled paper, and at least 50 percent of the fiber in our book paper is either unbleached or bleached using Totally Chlorine Free (TCF), Processed Chlorine Free (PCF), or Enhanced Elemental Chlorine Free (EECF) processes.

More information about the Bank's environmental philosophy can be found at http://crinfo.worldbank.org/wbcrinfo/node/4.

green
press
INITIATIVE